HOW TO EAT
like there's no tomorrow

also by Robert Elliott:

THE FOOD MAZE

Praise for The Food Maze

"Gifted with the intellect of a professional and the voice of a layman . . . gives the reader an immediately accessible guide to the workings of modern convenience culture."
The Ecologist

"Speaks in a style that is accessible, delivering a book that is a simple exercise in common sense."
Positive News

"An account billed 'for the common man', but written with uncommon intelligence."
Silvija Davidson, Slow Food

"A join-the-dots title, it will inspire you to make positive changes to the way you see the world."
The Green Parent

"This book acts as a guide . . . gives us a clear understanding of what our food is all about."
Ethical Living

"Writes with authority and passion about a subject that must concern us all."
Wye Valley AONB magazine

"This book will change the way you shop."
Wellbeing Magazine

And, from our inbox . . .

" . . . *essential reading for anyone remotely interested in food.*"

" . . . *absolutely absorbing, frightening, but reassuring and life-changing.*"

" . . . *Its powerful message has pricked my conscience on so many levels that I have already made some fundamental changes to the way I feed my family.*"

" . . . *a combination of frankness, humility, common sense and literary genius.*"

" . . . *radically changed the way we think about food – we now question everything we buy.*"

" . . . *I have not read another critical comment on the food industry which is so comprehensive, well researched, clear and passionate.*"

" . . . *a big thank you for such a well written and thought-provoking book.*"

" . . . *the personal anecdotes and writing style kept me gripped to the end.*"

About the author

Rob Elliott has pretty much been involved in food since the age of thirteen, when he took up the challenge of cooking for the family whilst his mother was in hospital. Over the years, his culinary experiences have ranged from cooking freshly caught mackerel over a campfire to catering virtually single-handedly for wedding receptions for 200 guests. Since 2002, he has pursued this interest in food at Aspen House in Herefordshire, a highly acclaimed award-winning B&B, which he runs with his partner, Sally Dean, whose understanding of nutrition goes far beyond her paper qualifications. Aspen House is the showcase for their joint ethos of using locally sourced food which is fresh, seasonal, grown to organic principles and uncontaminated by chemicals.

HOW TO EAT
like there's no tomorrow

Robert Elliott

Drawings by Chris Elliott

The Real Life Book Company Limited,

Hoarwithy,

Herefordshire, HR2 6QP.

Telephone 01432 840353

www.reallifepublishing.co.uk

© **Robert Elliott 2009**

ISBN 978-0-9558425-1-1

Cover design and Printed by
Orphans Press
Leominster, Herefordshire
United Kingdom
01568 612460

Printed on paper from sustainable sources

To my mother

Jadwiga Antonina Helena Wolanska

without whom I would never have understood
the true meaning of food

Recipes

CONTENTS

"Truth is ever to be found in simplicity, and not in the multiplicity and confusion of things."

Sir Isaac Newton

"If people let government decide what foods they eat and what medicines they take, their bodies will soon be in as sorry a state as are the souls of those who live under tyranny."

Thomas Jefferson

PREFACE

This is a book about food. But why, you may ask, do we need yet another book about food, when there are already so many out there? The answer, somewhat abstrusely perhaps, is precisely that: because there are so many. Ranging from books on the history of table manners and the etiquette of social dining to glossy recipe collections endorsed by celebrity chefs, to diatribes on the folly of eating meat, books about food take up miles of shelf space in our bookshops. I personally know of around a dozen bookshops that sell nothing but books about food – I am sure there must be more. Clearly, it is a popular subject, on which opinions alight like wasps on an overripe apple.

We must ask ourselves, therefore, why the subject is so fashionable that our interest in it has become obsessive, compulsively drawing us into the hype on new dietary or nutritional fads or the latest cookbooks, to say nothing of the TV shows that spawn them. Trapped between lust and loathing, we have become fearful of food, awed by its power over our health and the shape of our bodies. At the same time we remain beguiled by its seductiveness, its promise of illicit pleasure. For every cookery book that tempts us into guilty indulgence there is an equally powerful diet book that condemns the iniquity of pleasurable eating, chastising us for our wickedness and imposing on us through its pages an unsustainable regime to assuage the guilt and purge us of our lasciviousness.

And then of course there is science or, more accurately, pseudo-science. The scientific approach to food has grown with the same ominous relentlessness as the cancers and other diseases of civilisation from which science purports to free us. To many ordinary people, including me, there is something unnerving about the correlation between the two. More disturbingly, there are too many food scientists who seem oblivious to it. This in turn sets off more alarm bells.

Clearly, there is something very wrong here. And, like the proverbial elephant in the room, what is wrong is blindingly obvious once we are prepared to give it some attention. What we are all trying so hard to ignore is that industrial food is gradually killing us, and it is killing the planet. Moreover, our ability to understand this is severely impaired through our dissociation with food itself. Abdicating responsibility for the gathering of our own food, we are now so out of touch with what this entails that we no longer recognize what food is all about. The fundamental relationship between us and our food, which for centuries provided the foundation for societal and communal stability, has broken down, leaving us emotionally adrift and at the mercy of all the psychological elements threatening to swamp us.

Thus we have no idea whether or not to love food or loathe it. We know too little to be able to make effective judgements on what we are told by those upon whom we have conferred the authority to make food decisions on our behalf. In something akin to Alice's Wonderland, we eat foods which are bad for us, avoid foods which are good for us, crave foods forbidden to us and fear traditional foods demonised by those who profit from our uncertainties. When such confusions consume our thoughts, is it any wonder that there are so many books out there about food? Bookshop shelves bulge with cookery books and diet books, so that we can drive ourselves insane trying not to eat those delicious dishes we have just learned to cook.

We cannot let it go, this preoccupation with food, and therein lies my hope that we can extricate ourselves from this madness, and reclaim the relationship with our source of physical and spiritual sustenance. We cannot let it go because food is a primary force for every living thing, including us. In human terms, it should be the catalyst that binds us to nature more than anything else we do, forming a link between us and our environment. In all traditional agricultural societies, which would have included our own until relatively recently, food formed the core of community and was celebrated in sacred terms. In homage to Nature's bounty, human society displayed a true respect for the need to safeguard her fecundity, and we did our best to maintain a harmonious co-existence.

Now that has all gone. This humble recognition of our place in the greater realm of nature has been usurped by money and power. Corporate thinking sees the world and its resources as there for the taking. All of our fertile land mass, as well as the seas and oceans, have been enclosed, commercialised, privatised and thoroughly exploited for nothing more than monetary market value. The relentlessness of this conquest has seen corporate interest taking control of our seeds, plants and animal breeds, creating such a huge loss of biodiversity that all ecosystems on the planet are now under threat of collapse.

And so we come to the purpose of this book. There is an urgent need for us to revive our relationship with food and to rebuild our broken bonds with nature. Thankfully, we do live in a time of change, and many now recognise that there is a pressing requirement to relearn the lost skills of growing, cooking and eating. Many new titles are being published pointing the way to sustainable growing and real cooking, but there are surprisingly few books on the lost art of eating. Yet, in the act of eating is that implicit communion between humanity and nature as the source of our nourishment. In writing this book, it is my intention to examine why eating deserves a little respect, in the hope that you will find in these pages reason enough to see the need for all of us to change the way we eat.

Industrialisation of our food has created what is effectively an alien eating system, one to which our bodies are not adapted. In doing so, it has disrupted and damaged our health, laid waste our fertile lands right across the planet, decimated our global flora and fauna and blown gaping holes in the fragile, delicately balanced ecosystems which hold life together. Left to its own devices, industry will continue to do what it is programmed to do – exploit our natural resources for profit. But such a scenario is not inevitable. Many believe that we are at the beginning of a new age in history, one in which we humans finally come to accept that we might have a role as custodians of the Earth, our only Garden of Eden.

Our time is now, if there is to be any possibility of reversing the trend towards inevitable self-destruction. We must instigate change on an individual and personal level. So let this book be your guide and your counsellor in giving you time to think about the crumbling liaison with our food and to understand that, of all human connections, the one between us and our food is literally vital and is the one that we should, and can, fix. All other human and social relationships form the spokes that slot directly into this central hub. Food, that is to say real, wholesome, nutritious food, makes our social wheels turn smoothly.

In putting this book together, I have drawn on my own experiences in running a 'real food' B&B, Aspen House, with my partner, Sally Dean, whose nutritional expertise and understanding of food goes far beyond her paper qualifications. Our journey together at Aspen House has taken us from unrepentant supermarket shoppers to a higher level of understanding of what food is really all about. We have come to develop a philosophy that has changed our own lives for the better, and we found it surprisingly easy to do. The changes we made did not require any major upheaval of daily routine or any revolutionary thinking, unless it is true that eating real chocolate instead of cheap candy bars is in some way revolutionary.

The connections that each of us maintains with our wider environment is subject to the decisions we make. If our collective decision is to do nothing to alter the way we see our relationship with food, this would signal disaster for the ecological stability of the planet, inextricably linked as it is with the twin threats of Peak Oil and climate change. On the other hand, a collective decision to rethink the way we go about our lives can herald a reversal of harmful activity and a decrease in further destruction to our fragile ecosystems. And the power to swing the pendulum lies in our hands.

Though it may seem unlikely that a simple change could make any significant difference, history proves otherwise. Change is always worth the effort, and small increments of change can add up to something colossal. It could be argued that, in a democratic society, change requires the action of a large number of people but, it is also true that the simpler the action required to make the change, the more people will participate. To precipitate change requires one person to think differently enough to influence another, and thus the wave gathers momentum.

My hope is that what is written here will influence a change in you, and that you will be prompted to look differently at the act of eating, in the light of its far-reaching effects on the ecology of our planet. If a change in eating habits is accompanied by a personal reassessment of the nature of true nourishment in feeding the soul as well as the body, we will begin to understand the sacred value of life on this planet in its true holistic sense. Without such a change, our bond with our food will remain severed and the systems which currently provide us with an unending daily diet of industrial foods will continue to dominate. Thus the inexorable plunge towards a collapse of our species will remain virtually certain, and we will be able to predict at least one thing with eventual certainty – *there will be no tomorrow.*

Chapter One

Eat . . . naturally

I used to think my diet was pretty good. Avoiding what I considered to be junk food, I firmly believed that I was looking after myself and my family. Ten years ago, my old life collapsed, and I ended up eating alone most of the time. However, the eating habits I had become used to were still with me and were just that – habits. I ate as I had always eaten and still believed that my diet was exemplary.

At around that time, I was joined on the path of life by someone called Sally, whose world view seemed to coincide uncannily with my own. We walked together, sharing an interest in nature and a natural way of life, talking about food, health and wellbeing along the way. Three years later, we set out on the new adventure of running a B&B 'with a difference,' in other words, the kind of B&B we would want to stay in ourselves. From the start, we asked questions about food. Sally asked questions about my food, to which I replied defensively. It became clear that she was onto something though, and my erstwhile belief system regarding my sustenance began to crumble. Within five years of opening Aspen House, a new set of beliefs began to emerge and I found myself writing a book, *The Food Maze*, which describes this process in some detail. However, a brief recap here will not go amiss.

Looking back at a younger version of myself, I see that between the ages of twenty-something and about forty I was just another beer-drinking, tobacco-smoking headcase, with delusions of immortality and a penchant for tomato sandwiches that bordered on fetishism. I knew what was what, though, so I didn't smoke those nasty old cancer sticks that came in packs of twenty, accompanied by an aggressive fanfare of high-calibre marketing. I wasn't going to fall for all that hype – what, me? I was no victim of mass hysteria. So B&H and Embassy held no sway with me. I made my own bespoke cigarettes out of pure hand-rolled tobacco, using Rizla Wheetstraw papers (wheat straw – the natural killer, as I used to say).

It was the same with food. Virtually addicted to tomato sandwiches as a lunchtime snack, or indeed an anytime snack, I refused nevertheless to compromise on quality. I would buy my bread from the local baker and my tomatoes from the local greengrocer, substituting Canary tomatoes in the winter months. Unbeknown to me, however, was the fact that the bread, even though it was made by the local baker and was in a completely different league from the usual supermarket pap, was made from standard flour, bought in by the sackload from one of the big corporate flour millers. Made from monoculture wheat adulterated with pesticides, crushed in giant steel roller mills to remove its heart and soul, this wheat was nutritionally dead by the time it was made into the loaves I consumed with such unrestrained zeal. Every sandwich I ate compromised my immune system, already under attack from my other dubious habits. I didn't know that at the time and, to be fair to the baker, nor did he.

"Ask not what you can do for your country;
ask what's for lunch."

Orson Welles

When it came to buttering the slices, however, I can undoubtedly point the finger of blame at myself. As credulous as the next person when it comes to persuasive advertising, I fell for the butter scam. Proud of the fact that no one would ever catch me sliding down the

snake of gullibility, being taken in by the serpentine slickness of sly
admen, I nevertheless believed the propaganda about butter being bad
for me. Dutifully, I replaced butter with Flora, but the taste was so
dreadful that I graded up to Clover, persuading myself that its notably
yellow colour must surely deliver a taste that was just about acceptable,
so long as there wasn't very much of it and there was a good layer of
tomato between the slices of bread. Again, the chemical concoction of
factory-assembled processed ingredients stormed the ramparts of my
immune system. Oblivious as ever, I congratulated myself on bridging
that gap, not with Cadbury's Snack, but with a good healthy tomato
sandwich.

In blissful ignorance of the poor nutritional quality of my favourite
nibble, I continued to put away tomato sandwiches at an alarming rate,
rewarding myself for all this healthy eating with the occasional deep-
pan pizza or spicy take-away. I knew the latter were firmly in the junk
food category, but surely a little treat here and here would not go amiss.
The same reasoning was used every time I purchased a Twix bar, a Kit
Kat or a Cadbury's Flake . . .

Despite regular exercise, I was putting on weight and becoming
more and more lethargic. By the end of the '90s, I had reached the
stage whereby, if I stopped moving, I fell asleep. I could literally fall
asleep on my feet, and when I was awake I knew exactly what was
meant by the new buzz phrase, 'tired-all-the-time.' Feeling old before
my time, I tried to justify my condition by persuading myself that I was
indeed getting on a bit. Thus, in deeply philosophical mood, I would
sigh, collapse on the sofa, adjust my position to compensate for the
aches and pains in my back, my knees, my neck and my head, then
tuck into the tomato sandwiches I had made in order to give me a little
sustenance before tea. Then I would fall asleep.

Moving up inexorably to around three stones overweight, I was
concerned, but couldn't really identify what the problem might be. In
any case, if I stopped to think about it, I just fell asleep again. Weirdly,
when I went to bed, my sleep was somewhat restless. I put this down
to the fact that I had spent too long crashed out on the sofa before going
to bed. But then, I would wake up tired and yawn through my breakfast

of branflakes and semi-skimmed milk . . .with a little sprinkling of sugar, of course.

My eyesight started to deteriorate around that time. Again, I told myself that it was only to be expected, man of my age and all that. Plus, I was dead beat most of the time – surely that was bound to affect my eyes, wasn't it?

The situation had not really improved much by the time my life path met Sally's. In new-found companionship, we discovered the path we walked led to Aspen House, the B&B business that we took over in 2002. Moving in with a man she knew nothing about and with whom she intended to run a relatively stressful business was something that Sally was warned about by her best friend. But she went ahead and did it anyway. Shortly after this step into the unknown, she realised what she had taken on – someone who, on a bad day, could barely put one foot in front of the other. Something had to be done.

With an extensive understanding of nutrition, Sally quite rightly diagnosed that my problem was likely to be diet-based. She talked to her friend at work and, before I knew what was happening, I became a test case and found myself lying on my back quietly going to sleep while Sally and her friend talked in subdued tones about food intolerance. The upshot of this brief but restful session was that I was informed that I'd 'got candida'. This, it transpired, was a yeast that all of us have living quite happily in our gut but which, in my case, had got out of control, had broken ranks and was now running amok creating all kinds of mayhem.

Put in less flippant terms, it appeared that I had helped this candida to break out by feeding it all its favourite foods, such as sugar, yeast and starch. My diet was changed to create a 'candida starvation plan'. It worked. Further testing a few months later revealed that it was in retreat. Sadly for me, I had been asked to cut out wheat, yeast, dairy products, as well as things like mushrooms (another fungus!) and dried fruits (not a fungus, but with fungus on the surface, as well as a high sugar content). Replacing yeasted wheat bread with rye sourdough was something I could cope with, but substituting soya milk for cow's milk was a bit grim. Worse than that, I was being asked to use Pure spread as a butter substitute. In my tomato sandwich fetish days, I had just about put up with Clover spread, but this Pure stuff was foul. However, I needed to get my candida under control, so I simply came to terms with it.

Some time later, Sally and I experienced a memorable eureka moment. Sally had been reading about the benefits of unpasteurised milk from cows raised on traditional pasture. She felt it would be worth testing me on it, so we managed to track some down, and the test was applied. Instead of my usual negative reaction to milk, which had become the norm ever since I had first been tested, the reaction this time was very positive.

It took a while to work forward from this point to the obvious but politically incorrect conclusion that a diagnosis of 'wheat and dairy intolerance' (the mantra of the 21st Century) was far too simplistic. Further testing of a much more specific nature showed that my body was reacting negatively, not simply to wheat and dairy, but to *processed* or adulterated wheat and dairy. As testing continued, it became evident that I was having a bad reaction towards *anything* processed, but an extremely favourable reaction towards anything natural.

Of course, this would all be roundly condemned by a scientific tradition that demands empirical double-blind proof for everything. However, we are not talking peer-reviewed scientific papers here – just down-to-earth common sense. Once we had reached this conclusion, I simply cut out all processed and adulterated foodstuffs and reverted to a 100% natural diet.

Four years on, and we flash forward to the present day. Many things have happened to me – all of them good. For a start, I have had only one cold in those four years, and that was in the first year. I have lost all the little aches, pains and general niggles that become part of life for people of a certain age. My teeth, often in the past wavering between sensitive and troublesome, no longer give me any bother. Headaches, sniffles and an itchy nose have all gone. Fingernails that used to split and flake constantly, especially with the amount of washing up involved in running a B&B, are now so strong that I can cut them only if they have been soaked for a while in hot water.

The spectacles that I own, the purchase of which I had to succumb to when my sight became so bad that I was unable to see any stage performance clearly, have now been in the drawer for three years. I lost weight initially, and then stabilised at a weight I have not been able to achieve since my twenties – a weight which has remained constant over the last three years, despite a diet to which many people would hold up the burning cross of received wisdom. My heartbeat, blood pressure, cholesterol count and all those other indicators so beloved of the medical profession in assessing our viability as vital beings, remain constantly stable. Yet I now enjoy a diet that would have many medics shiver in horror.

All the processed foods have gone. No Weetabix, Branflakes or commodity milk – in their place porridge or overnight soaked muesli with unpasteurised milk. No Flora, Clover or Pure on my toast, just gorgeous farmhouse butter from a dairy that runs a small pasture-fed herd. When we cook pork, it is the best truly free-range pork we can find and the crackling, covering a thick band of melt-in-the-mouth fat, is perfect every time. This splendid crackling is devoured along with the meat and fat – all far too tasty to push to one side of the plate. I don't have many tomato sandwiches these days, but that is partly because I will now eat only tomatoes grown in season and outdoors, because all the usual varieties are so bland. Even Canary tomatoes, those firm bright red orbs that used to sing out to me in the depths of winter are now pretty much indistinguishable from the other monocultured products. I find that the tomato, in season and straight from the garden, is really the only kind of tomato worth eating, and mostly it is far more satisfying to eat it on its own than to muffle its flavour with bread. Having said that, if I do make a tomato sandwich these days, I go to some trouble, as you will see below. Mostly though, the need for intermittent snacks has evaporated. A breakfast of porridge followed by two poached eggs on home made sourdough rye toast is enough to keep me going on all cylinders for the best part of the day. I have more energy than I have had for well over a decade, and I can sit in front of the computer for hours without falling asleep. Four years ago, I would last about ten minutes.

A proper tomato sandwich

You will need some ripe home-grown tomatoes (dead easy – all you need is a hanging basket, some tomato plants and a warm sunny spot to hang the basket), some fresh home-made bread, real butter, some home-made mayonnaise, a few fresh mint leaves (yes, you can grow this in a pot) plus some good quality sea salt and freshly ground black pepper.

I am not going to tell you how to make the sandwich, but I will tell you how to make the mayonnaise, because it breaks my heart to see so much poor quality industrial mayonnaise sitting on supermarket shelves, and the real thing is not Hellmans but something you make at home in about five minutes.

For the mayonnaise, you will need 2 fresh organic eggs, a teaspoon of Dijon mustard, a pinch of fine sea salt, a couple of grinds of black pepper, a tablespoon of white wine or cider vinegar and half a pint of extra virgin olive oil.

Separate the eggs, putting the yolks in a bowl and saving the whites to do something with later [e.g. making meringues]. Add the mustard, salt and pepper to the egg yolks and then get out the electric hand whisk. As you beat the egg yolks on medium speed, gradually dribble in the oil, making sure it is thoroughly whipped as you go. You don't need to add the oil a drop at a time. You just need to ensure that it is mixed thoroughly, and you can gradually increase the speed with which you add the oil as the quantity of mayonnaise grows, but never add it more quickly than a steady trickle.

Halfway through the quantity of oil, you will find that your mixture is very thick. Add some vinegar at this point and whisk it again, then carry on trickling the oil in. You should find that, by the time you have used all the oil and all the vinegar, you have a perfectly smooth, soft, delicious mayonnaise that will proclaim to your tastebuds that this is how this alchemic culinary wonder should taste.

If at any point the mixture splits, just crack two more eggs yolks into a clean bowl and gradually beat in the curdled mixture. You will find that it will turn into mayonnaise that will simply be that bit creamier. If you can keep it that long, this should last for a couple of weeks in the fridge.

Best of all, I have developed a clearer understanding of food. I plainly see the utter stupidity of following this diet or that, or hooking up to the hype on the latest superfood. I can find no taste in the products of the highly processed foodstuffs industry – factory chocolate tastes of nothing except sugar and additives. Sugar, that white addictive substance that glitters alluringly as it drops off a spoon into a steaming cup of tea, holds no appeal for me now. To me, it tastes of what it is, refined sucrose, unnatural and sickly sweet. I now taste nature's sweetness – the subtle sweetness in fresh onions, potatoes or carrots. Even a freshly cut cabbage has a sweetness that I never would have believed is there.

My previous heavy indulgence in those things that caused me damage, those unsuspected debased products of food factories, has left me wary, but with a clear memory of what makes such comestibles so appealing to the taste buds. I treat these with a respect for their seductive powers, though I still view wheat with suspicion. However, the idea of relaxing with a cup of espresso coffee and a home made scone in one of our favourite coffee shops is very appealing, so I allow myself that pleasure, but only twice a week, as an indulgence. Never did coffee taste as good as it does when you know the next one is four days away! And the odd scone here and there is hardly comparable to my previous level of wheat consumption. In some places, we even have the bonus of the scones being made with good flour.

Although I think I have a long way to go before being able to claim a truly natural relationship with food, I can quite definitely say that there is an element of Zen in what both Sally and I do now, and Aspen House has become more than just a B&B. I have no fear of food and I have no cravings. Eating is a positive delight, as is the preparation and growing of food. I eat what is available locally and seasonally, and as fresh as possible. A resurrected fondness for wild food sees us out gathering hedge mustard, wild garlic and other greenstuffs to supplement the first green salads of spring. Instinct tells me if there is anything lacking in my diet. Thus I feel very much in tune with my body's needs. Theoretically, nothing is prohibited in my diet. I certainly eat what I like, but it no longer includes all those industrialised foodstuffs. These are unnatural foods and that is exactly how they taste to me now. Losing my dependence on them has literally changed my life – don't you just love that phrase?

Nature's food

For those aspiring to bring a little touch of Zen into their lives, there is a gift from nature so easily overlooked, and that is wild food. Though we might be familiar with the idea of gathering hazelnuts, blackberries or mushrooms in late summer, many wild green plants are delicious, and those that appear in the spring can be a welcome nutritional boost to a seasonal salad.

Though urban dwellers might say that such things are unavailable to them, I would say that they might be surprised at what grows along footpaths, commons or local parks and woods, perhaps even in the back garden. Let's face it, nettles are seen everywhere and they can be made into an excellent soup with the addition of a few potatoes, some good home made stock and a bit of seasoning.

Other equally common plants, such as wild garlic, hedge mustard (more endearingly called Jack-by-the-Hedge) and the ubiquitous dandelion, are more abundant than most of us realise, and they taste wonderful in a salad. I would recommend getting hold of a copy of *Food For Free* by Richard Mabey, or something similar, and use it as a reference next time you go out for a walk. Your salads will move into a different league!

My journey has taken me from a belief system in which I had good faith to an understanding that all is not actually as I perceived it to be. Worse than that, it would seem that, although my penchant for tomatoes seemed perfectly natural to me at the time, I have learned that 'natural' is a word with a chimeric quality. In this opening chapter, it would seem appropriate that we look at this idea a little more closely.

Most of us, with some justification, would be appalled by the implication that we are not eating naturally. However, it is true to say that there is more than one definition of what is meant by 'natural' and 'naturally'. Of the thirteen separate meanings for 'natural' recorded in my Oxford Reference Dictionary, the one with which I am working here is the primary one. This describes 'natural' as 'existing or caused by nature: not artificial.' For the sake of clarity, we should also define 'artificial'. Here we find two principal meanings: 1) produced by human art or effort rather than originating *naturally*; 2) not real; imitation; fake. I hardly think I need to elaborate further – I am sure we all know what is meant by 'not real', 'imitation' and 'fake.' To round off this little stroll through the dictionary, 'naturally' is defined as 'in a natural manner.'

At the risk of going round in circles, we could say the phrase, 'in a natural manner', is easily interpreted as 'doing what comes naturally'. However, these are chameleon words with many possible interpretations, changing their meaning to suit different conditions. Thus, when applying the words to eating, it appears that, for many people, eating naturally could mean grazing on snacks throughout the day, gobbling down a couple of Big Macs, eating on the move or heating up something in the microwave after getting home from work. It is hardly surprising that all of these are understood to be completely natural, considering the billions of pounds of advertising money that has been spent over the decades, persuading us that this is how we should be eating. We have been guided towards the increasing number of junk food fuelling stations and supermarkets to obtain the foodstuffs we are persuaded to buy. For the corporations involved, this campaign has been spectacularly successful. Around 80% of what we purchase to eat at home is now brought to us by the Big Four UK supermarkets

(Tesco, Asda, Morrisons and Sainsbury's).

Thus, for the majority, obtaining our daily sustenance has become nothing more than a trip to the local out-of-town superstore to trawl the aisles, load the trolley, take it to the checkout and transport it home by car in land-clogging plastic bags. Dispassionately observed by a zoologist from another universe, this would appear to be a somewhat bizarre behaviour pattern, but it is now so commonplace that it is seen as completely natural. Those who indulge in this strange ritual defend it vociferously. As far as they are concerned, it is just shopping for food, and we all do it. Even to an anthropologist, this might seem to be nothing more than Man, the hunter-gatherer, projected into the 21st Century and finding his food in the most efficient way that the modern world will allow.

Although it is true that we are essentially no more than one of the many species on this planet, and are therefore, by definition, natural, and thus are doing only what comes naturally, it is far too simplistic an argument to say that we are merely acting as we are programmed to act. This kind of reasoning accepts without question that absolutely anything we do can be seen as a demonstration of natural behaviour. By that claim, exploiting the planet's finite resources, or creating indestructible nuclear waste, is fine, because it is no more than Man acting naturally. Killing millions of bison just for fun on the great plains of North America is presumably okay too, as is the killing of millions of Jews in Nazi concentration camps. Such an argument would say that all this is simply part of what we do. It can all be called natural behaviour, so there is nothing to worry about and we should stop agonising, get on with our lives and get on down to the supermarket for our next trolley load.

Others, including me, oppose this argument. We might well be just another species but, for whatever reason, we have been given the ability to think and behave in a way unique amongst all the species on Earth. We can think in the abstract, and process those thoughts in speech, pictures, prose and poetry, in thousands of different languages and dialects. We can reason, philosophise, argue and pontificate. Our thinking also translates into practicality. Beyond the abilities of all other species, we have built a vast and hugely complex machine-driven society, with computers that do millions of calculations per second, fighter jets that travel in excess of 2000 mph and cars that are built by robots. Pretty clever, you might say. But our high-powered brains carry fatal flaws. Like the Internet (another of Man's Marvellous Manifestations), our brains let everything in, good and bad alike. Because of our intellect and our powers of reasoning, we can blur the distinctions between these two opposites, to the extent that we can easily persuade ourselves that good is bad and bad is good, if it suits us to do so.

The idea of collecting items of pre-packaged food amidst hordes of strangers to whom we don't speak, in an artificially lit warehouse full of the colourfully wrapped, nutritionally depleted products of profit-driven factories has been sold to us as being a life-enhancing concept. This is simply because advertising psychology has identified that we will respond positively to the two clarion calls of convenience and cheapness. Because we are all for an easy life, we remain convinced that we are behaving quite naturally. However, the only natural elements in all this are the basic human instincts which have been manipulated by the marketing industry to lead us into a behaviour pattern that suits their need for predictable and profitable bottom-line results. Good for profitability, but bad for us, it has been argued by Barry Groves in his book, *Trick and Treat,* that 90% of what is now available in the supermarket is so unnatural that it is technically unfit for human consumption.

> *"Fake food – I mean those patented substances chemically flavoured and mechanically bulked out to kill the appetite and deceive the gut – is unnatural, almost immoral, a bane to good eating and good cooking."*
>
> Julia Child [1912 – 2004]

Fake food, or what I call processed or industrial food, can be visually obvious, especially in places like motorway service areas, but it also comes in some pretty effective disguises. To list some of them:

- Weetabix, Shredded Wheat and other 'healthy' cereals – made from monocultured grain, cooked, extruded and shaped.

- Low-fat 'healthy' products like spreads and pro-biotic drinks – a concoction of factory ingredients and/or containing too much sugar.

- Sugar itself – processed and refined cane or beet sugar is an unnatural 'food' that plays havoc with our hormones.

- Milk – if it is skimmed or semi-skimmed, standardised, pasteurised and homogenised commodity milk, it is over-processed. The nearest we can get to real milk through the major retailers is organic whole milk.

- Soya – often consumed in the form of milk by those who are 'dairy intolerant', but all soya products, unless fermented, are difficult for our bodies to deal with.

- Bread and flour – the standard white (or brown) sliced loaf should probably carry a government health warning, and standard white flour is quite simply a dead powder.

- Citrus juices – processed from fruit concentrates and an unnatural way to consume the juice of a fruit.

- Battery chicken – not just cheap chicken, but processed and manipulated to reach a particular weight in a particular number of days.

- Supermarket fruit and vegetables – mostly from chemically supported monocultures, these might look real enough, but are nutritionally depleted.

On the long journey of our evolution, we accumulated knowledge of which foods, particularly plants, were good to eat and which were poisonous, or how to prepare and cook certain plants in order to make them harmless. As a child, I remember walking with my grandfather in the fields behind his farm. As we walked, he would point out the kinds of things that might interest a small boy – a hawk's nest, a fox's footprint, the direction in which a mole was tunnelling. I remember crossing a stream where the water was shallow and green plants grew in profusion. Grandpa bent down and picked two stalks.

"This is watercress, and good to eat," he said, offering me some.

"This other one," he added, comparing the two, "looks like watercress, but it is poisonous. See the difference and make sure you know which is which."

Knowledge like this has all but gone. We think we are eating naturally, but we are not. We have lost touch with our food. How many people know anything about wild foods these days? There are still experts out there, but our general knowledge on such things is sparse. We have no use for it any more, now that the supermarkets take care of our every need. Herein lies real danger, because the food industry tells us only what it wants us to know. It tells us nothing about additives and artificial ingredients unless legislation makes it compulsory to do so. But legislation does not cover it all, and there is much that slips into our diet by stealth.

Symptomatic of a life which is becoming less natural as time goes on, 21st Century food shopping, and the subsequent consumption of what has been brought home, is increasingly a de-humanising experience, to the extent that we run the risk of eventually becoming completely de-natured, compliant slaves to the machine age we have created. Undoubtedly, this is a grim prognosis for the brightest species on the planet. However, there is one trait common to all species on Earth, including *homo sapiens* – the survival instinct. This, the optimists will tell you, is what will bring us back from the brink before it is too late. Certainly there are signs that an increasing number of people feel uneasy about the life we live. Some admit to confusion, others ask questions, seeking explanations for their disquiet and unrest.

Personally I am of an optimistic frame of mind. I see no harm in directing this fresh wind of change to fan into flame these sparks of dissent. We might be running the risk of a conflagration ripping through the dry scrubland of received wisdom, but in its place new shoots of understanding will undoubtedly spring forth.

One such shoot is already growing taller by the day, and that is the awareness that the industrial age has damaged our food. This awareness is as old as the industrial age itself. As long ago as 1820, Frederick Accum published a book entitled *A Treatise on Adulterations of Food and Culinary Poisons*, detailing his concerns that food was being degraded by new production methods and unscrupulous entrepreneurs whose overriding motivation was the creation of profit. It is unsettling to think that nearly 200 years have passed since Accum demonstrated sufficient concern about being cheated by the food industry that he was prompted to publish his findings in a book. What is so disturbing is that today nothing much has changed, except for the fact that the food industry is now far more cute about how it presents itself, relying on its financial power to buy the most persuasive advertising as well as the sanction of compliant governments.

Voices of reason have been heard from time to time over the last two hundred years, but they have been dismissed by the rich and powerful as cranky prophets of doom. The huge wheels of the industrial food industry have turned without hindrance since Accum's time, and have become so much part of modern life that most people barely notice the ruts they make as they trundle through our cultural traditions and culinary heritage. We are now in the midst of a nutritional desert, where every natural food that has sustained us for millennia is challenged by an artificial alternative, sold to us by an ever more sophisticated marketing industry whose understanding of human psychology is often greater than some of our leading medical specialists.

Our food has always been tampered with, of course. Back in the 13th century, the *Assize of Bread and Ale* was drawn up as the first piece of legislation to regulate the production and sale of food, setting down guidelines for bakers and brewers to reduce the incidence of cheating.

Once the Industrial Revolution picked up speed, however, tampering with our food literally became big business. Driven by a desire for wealth, the new industrial pioneers became ever more ingenious in devising ways of minimising costs and maximising profits. In the food industry, this generally meant automating production processes and compromising on quality ingredients either by removing them from the process or replacing them with an artificial alternative.

As the food factories became bigger, so the burgeoning industry spawned ancillary industries producing the synthetic additives necessary to bring down the basic costs of production. This is not some long-forgotten nightmare of the smoke-blackened Victorian world described so eloquently by Charles Dickens, or even a scene from the grimy gloomy Industrial North of George Orwell's Road to Wigan Pier. This is the world we live in today. A world in which our food is tainted with cheap artificial additives and toxic ingredients. In many cases, it contains practically zero nutrition. And, with a flashy smile from the industry's slick salesmen, we have been sold the idea that all of this is perfectly natural. Compounding the deceit, we have been told, for at least the last fifty years, that this factory fodder is better than natural – it has been 'scientifically proved' to be exactly what we need to be the fittest and healthiest human beings that ever lived. It seems strange, therefore, that we appear to be dropping like flies.

The malfunctions that currently affect our bodily systems are comparatively new. So new, in fact, that they have been grouped under their own special name of 'the diseases of civilisation.' More accurately described as the diseases of industrialisation, their rate of incidence has increased in line with our expanding industrial economy. Degenerative diseases, such as heart disease, diabetes, obesity, asthma and a proliferation of every type of cancer, show no signs of being kept in check, despite the billions in research funding and a burgeoning pharmaceutical industry. Governments spout platitudes, medical establishments give assurances and the drug industry says, "Don't worry, we have the solution." Yet, the one thing that remains certain is that we are sick.

Throughout the developed world, we are laid low by the diseases of industrialisation, whilst in the heavily exploited so-called Third World an unacceptably high number of people, if they are not actually starving, are dying from preventable diseases, brought to this unhappy state by avaricious corporations and the selfishness of egocentric global organisations such as the World Bank, the International Monetary Fund and the World Trade Organisation.

By writing this, I run the risk of sounding political, and maybe that is uncalled for in a book about food and eating. Sadly though, food today is inextricably tied up with politics, and it would be easy to expand on this theme, but the politics of food really is a different story that has been told more than adequately by others. The question which concerns us here is whether or not our modern eating habits can be described as natural. Those powerful factory producers, agri-businesses and their retail distribution network, the supermarkets, assure us that everything we do is perfectly natural. Moreover, they like to tell us that our natural behaviour makes us a fickle lot and difficult to please, and that they all spare no effort in delivering to us what we want. This is a long way from the truth.

In reality, all corporations are run by hard-as-nails management teams with one eye on the competition and the other eye on the shareholders. They create a world that suits them and establishes the best opportunity to stay ahead of the competition whilst delivering dividends to their shareholders. Whether or not they do harm to our food in pursuit of these two goals is a secondary consideration. Research departments are there to provide the 'scientifically proven' reports used by the corporations to sell their products. After that, their marketing departments and advertising agencies can fool us into thinking that we are being taken care of, the question of the adulteration of food becomes no more than an irritating diversion, the discussion of which in the media is to be avoided. So long as harmful stories can be kept out of the media, harmful food is not something big business worries about. We are the ones who must worry. We have been taken in by the food industry and we have allowed them to take charge of our food. Delegating responsibility for our food to big business was all too easy, soothed as we were by the soporific tones of the admen. Now we must count the cost of this entrustment.

By allowing others to put themselves in charge of the procurement and distribution of our food, we have inadvertently created a demon that has wreaked havoc on us and the planet on which we live. But we all make mistakes – just look at me and my tomato sandwiches. The usefulness of mistakes is that we can learn from them. So, what have we learned? Well, it could be argued that we have learned only how to eat unnaturally. For every natural food that we once enjoyed, there is now an artificial alternative.

More worryingly, these fakes have been sold to us as the real deal, demonising our traditional foods in the process. Virtually all of our natural food that has been taken up by the food industry has now been tampered with, and the fungus-like tentacles of industrialisation have tainted everything, even staples such as bread, dairy products, meat, vegetables and fruit. Chemicals pollute everything that is intensively grown or reared, antibiotics and growth promoters enter our food chains and artificial additives abound, contributing to the disruption and breakdown of our delicately balanced internal systems. The corporate approach to food has hijacked all attempts so far to stand against it and provide a clean alternative to dirty factory food. Thus it becomes increasingly difficult even to trust terms such as 'fresh', 'organic' or 'local'. The corporations have come up with their own versions of these and other terms, even to the extent of surreptitiously slipping 'organic pot noodle' into the marketplace for a time. We are living in a world where nutrition is in conflict with profit – and profit has been steadily gaining ground in this battle. But, with common sense and knowledge on our side, we could yet turn the tide.

With both common sense and knowledge comes the understanding that everything we have been told about the benefits of eating industrial foods is wrong. Factory food is quite simply bad for us. Despite the fact that it has been sold to us as the healthy option, common sense should tell us that this is risible. How can some industrial product, such as *Flora Pro-activ* for example, be better for us than its natural equivalent? Think about it. Stand back and look at it dispassionately. And now try to persuade yourself, without the aid of the adman's suggestive whisperings, that a product made in a factory, using a combination of artificial ingredients to replace a simple food that comes to us from nature, is going to be healthier for us. Ridiculous, isn't it? So ridiculous, in fact, that it is not difficult to conclude that what we take for granted today as being normal and natural is neither.

Thus the zenith of this particular learning curve is the realisation that we should return to something which can truly be described as 'eating naturally' while we still have a chance to do so. We must reject industrialised, factory-produced, intensively grown food in favour of foods that come to us as the untainted gifts of nature. Factory food, being nutritionally depleted, is inadequate and thus is bad for our health, and the steady increase in degenerative diseases over the last 150 years is, for me and Sally at least, proof of that.

Chapter Two

Eat . . . healthily

To eat healthily, we must eat naturally, and so we must ask ourselves how naturally are we eating. According to a certain Japanese farmer, Masanobu Fukuoka (who died in 2008 at the age of 95), natural eating is so simple that we find it hard to grasp. But then, Fukuoka had taken the whole idea of natural eating to its logical conclusion.

As much a philosopher as he was a farmer, his approach to life was pure Zen, as described so eloquently in his books *The One-Straw Revolution* and *The Natural Way of Farming*. During his life, the essence of natural food for Fukuoka was the rice, vegetables and fruit that he produced without disturbing the ground in which it grew. Done as much to prove a point to those addicted to chemical farming as to demonstrate the Zen approach to farming, Fukuoka's ground didn't see a plough for 25 years. He truly was an accomplished exponent of the art of living and eating naturally. For him, the zenith of eating naturally and healthily is to eat 'without thinking,' to eat intuitively from what is available in the immediate vicinity, in season and in tune with nature.

To test the idea of eating healthily, try out a little experiment which Sally and I learned to use when we went out shopping. Next time you have something to eat, ask yourself, "Where has this come from and how has it been produced?" It doesn't matter what it is, whether it is a chocolate bar, a packet of crisps, a bowl of breakfast cereal, a home made casserole or a restaurant meal. The question is still pertinent. If the answer tells you that what you are eating is the result of some factory process, then you can safely assume the product is nutritionally empty and will probably also contain something harmful, even if it is only a shot of artificial colouring or a dose of preservative. In the case of the home made casserole, we should ask ourselves where the basic ingredients have come from. If the meat or vegetables have come from the supermarket, then it's a safe bet that they will be nutritionally depleted, even if labelled as organic. As for the restaurant meal, this line of questioning certainly throws into sharp relief how very few eating establishments are dedicated to the provision of food that is unadulterated, fresh, seasonal and local – the four criteria by which Sally and I now judge the nutritional quality of all that we eat. As awareness grows, so eating out becomes more of a challenge. In the true nature of all challenges, however, this should mean 'difficult but not impossible.'

As an author, I sense that I might be sailing into turbulent waters. I may be accused of taking an elitist stance, of making it impossible for anyone to go out and buy anything to eat at all. What I say in my own defence is that I report only what I find and that I too am concerned with the difficulty in finding real food. The best produce is often hidden in the long shadows thrown by the 'friendly neighbourhood supermarket'. It can be difficult to see and, when you do see it, it may be limited to a few stalls at a Farmer's Market. Or it may have to be accessed via a veg-box scheme. Finding the best produce in a world dominated by giant retailers requires some effort.

Local enterprise is initially stifled and then choked to death by the grip of a large retail outlet in the vicinity. However benign the big retailers would like us to believe they are, the truth is that their presence in any given area is actually the kiss of death for smaller businesses. These independents wither and die, and the best local produce that they may have sold at one time disappears with them, leaving us unable to source it without some difficulty. The easier option is not to bother.

Each of us is an individual, and each of us is entitled to make a personal choice. If your personal choice is to decide that it is just too much trouble to source real food, then stop reading now, because the rest of this book will simply be a waste of your time. If, on the other hand, you can see the sense in feeding your body something nutritious and healthy, whilst regaining the true essence of eating as a fundamental human experience, you will no doubt understand that the ideal is difficult to achieve, but worth the effort. So I invite you to read on.

'Twas ever thus . . .

> *"Such is the audacity of man, that he hath learned*
> *to counterfeit Nature, yea, and is so bold as to challenge*
> *her in her work."*
> Pliny the Elder, *The Natural History*,
> translated by Philemon Holland

To demonstrate how difficult it can be to find real food, or even to understand fully what it actually is, let us go back to *Flora pro-activ* for a moment. Having given it a passing mention in Chapter One, I want to spend some time on the whole idea behind it and what such a product represents, because it illustrates the point I am trying to make. Despite the polemic tone, I am going to put this under the microscope and use it as a symbol of exactly what we are being sold in place of the natural foods that are the bedrock of health, but I have no intention of spending more time than is necessary in this kind of analytical thought throughout the rest of the book.

Flora pro-activ is a branded factory product that is part of a range of what is the absolute latest in artificial 'designer foods', the so-called nutriceuticals – foods that perform some kind of supposed health-giving function. In this case, the function is to lower cholesterol. Immediately, a problem is raised with this idea, and the problem concerns cholesterol itself. There is a massively powerful industry out there, involving food and pharmaceutical drugs, that is making billions of pounds of profit out of the idea that cholesterol is bad for us, and that lowering cholesterol is an ideal towards which we should all strive. This idea could well turn out to be one of the greatest sleights-of-hand that has ever been foisted on us.

Contrary to what is generally believed about cholesterol, there are numerous books, scientific papers, learned studies and academic research programmes that have given us a huge amount of data firmly establishing cholesterol as one of the good guys. Cholesterol is involved in repair work to damaged cells. Its presence at the site of arterial damage is no more an indicator of offence than the presence of police at a crime scene is an indication that the police perpetrated the crime. It is remarkable how surreal society has become as a result of looking at so many things in this topsy-turvy way and creating what amount to 'urban myths'. In the case of cholesterol, the myth is that it is responsible for heart disease and furred arteries. This has grown out of flawed research and a poor understanding of the role of cholesterol, but the myth has been greedily pounced on by a drugs industry hungry for profit. And now the food industry has joined in. Together they form a lobby powerful enough to suppress any erudite claims that cholesterol is not the demon it is made out to be.

When it comes to food and health, many such myths and misunderstandings persist. For instance, there was the vegetarian staying at Aspen House who said, "It's not that I particularly want to eat vegetables, but meat is so bad for you, isn't it?" At one time or another over the last half century, it is quite likely that all of the natural foods that have sustained us for millennia have been condemned by the new Food Police. Certainly, many people today live in fear of red meat, eggs, cheese, cream, butter and whole milk. The root cause of this fear is the message that all these real foods contain saturated fats (except for eggs, which are roundly condemned in their own right as cholesterol time bombs), the inference being that the consumption of saturated fats will have us all dropping like flies with seized hearts and clogged arteries. The medical profession, the media and, most of all, the manufacturers of low-fat substitutes for real food, remind us almost daily that we all live in mortal danger if we allow saturated fats to creep into our diet, citing the rising incidence of heart disease and hardening arteries as irrefutable proof that they are right.

If we had been decimated with heart disease during the first part of the 20th Century, or even back into the 19th Century and beyond, and subsequently the medical profession during the latter half of the 20th Century had said, "Well, we have been laid low by this disease for the last 100 years, but finally we have found out what causes it," then I would accept what I am being told. But this is not the case. The case is that, prior to the 1950s, heart disease was not the epidemic it is today. Also the incidence of heart disease rises year by year and has done so since the '50s or thereabouts – precisely the same period of time that we have been moving away from traditional foods and consuming more factory products. To me, layman that I am, logic and common sense tell me that these two ideas, heart disease and industrial food, are linked.

Since the human race first cast a shadow across the land, its members have sought sustenance from the Earth in order to maintain life and procreate the species. We have continued to do this over millennia, gradually learning new skills in order to facilitate the task of food procurement. We have thrived, and our numbers now run into billions. Despite the refinements made possible by the introduction of farming, agriculture and the culinary arts, the basic foodstuffs that have sustained us have changed little over the ages. Vegetables, fruit, grains, seeds and a whole range of products derived from animals have enabled us to reproduce succeeding generations very successfully.

Then suddenly, over the last couple of generations or so, a new blueprint for survival has been laid out on the drawing board. This plan dismisses all that has gone before. Out with the old, in with the new. We have been told that many of those natural foods (mainly those derived from animals) are to be avoided, that they will draw us unwittingly into disease and death. Butter, whole milk, cheese, beef fat – killers all! The vehement hysteria with which these foods are condemned sounds to me too much like the madness that condemned so many innocent women to death in the witch hunts of the 17th Century. It appears that Matthew Hopkins, the Witchfinder General, is alive and well and is now the CEO of a food factory making low-fat spreads . . .

This book is not about the history of medical research, or a treatise on the Puritan excesses of 17th Century England, but if you are keen to know more, begin your journey to the centre of truth about cholesterol with *The Great Cholesterol Con* by Dr Malcolm Kendrick (an easy-to-follow read) and then move on to *What Doctors Don't Tell You* by Lynne McTaggart. *Trick and Treat* by Barry Groves is very comprehensively referenced and, for a more academic read, try *The Cholesterol Myths* by Dr Uffe Ravnskov, always assuming you can find a copy of this scarce book. After that, there are many more to choose from. And they will all tell you the same thing. They will tell you that there was a time when it was difficult to prove the connection between high cholesterol and an increased risk of heart disease, and that research into the idea was inconclusive. Then along came the pharmaceutical company, Merck, with a new cholesterol-lowering drug called lovastatin, launched in 1987 in a fanfare of publicity that sold the drug as the eighth wonder of the world. The statin revolution was upon us, and the pharmaceutical companies had hit the jackpot. Having no wish to kill this golden goose, Big Pharma began marketing this statin lifesaver, and the other versions that followed it, with the enthusiasm of a Victorian quack doctor. If statins were simply examples of some harmless snake oil concoction, there would be no issue here. After all, our gullible species has a history of parting with good money for dubious preparations. But those who challenge the cholesterol myth point out that statins are actually dangerous because of the physical and emotional side effects.

Nevertheless, the medical profession and the media easily swallowed the story, and the biggest industrial food giants, pound signs in their eyes, jumped in without prompting. On this bandwagon, the company that produces Flora, that global giant, Unilever, rides high, singing the anti-cholesterol message from the rooftops and getting into some serious sponsorship, such as the London Marathon. This, and the 'healthy heart' message that goes with it, is truly bizarre, considering that Flora is a factory product and, as Pat Thomas, the editor of *The Ecologist* points out (01/11/06), its combination of ingredients, mixed during the factory process, is far from healthy. Even if you accept the myth that cholesterol must be lowered at all costs, the ingredients in *Flora pro-activ* are not what you want to be spreading on your toast.

Flora pro-activ contains a high percentage of plant-based fats known as plant sterols, which some medical research shows can reduce the level of cholesterol in the blood. However, leaving aside any other issues, including the fact that we can get all the sterols we need from vegetables, fruit, nuts and seeds, the plant sterols in these modern spreads are not in their natural state. Because they are not freely soluble in oils and fats, these sterols are firstly hydrogenated and then compounded (esterified) with other fatty acids to enable them to mix better in the spread.

Then we come to the pseudo-hormonal effect of these modified sterols. A short time before they were given FDA (US Food and Drug Administration) approval, a research paper from Sweden stated in 1998, "further studies are required of [their] phyto-oestrogenic and endocrine effects, and [their] effects on growing children, particularly regarding subsequent fertility in boys." Though largely ignored by an industry that finds these products so lucrative, studies such as this one have resulted in a legal requirement for Flora and other sterol-containing products to carry the warning that pregnant and breastfeeding women and young children 'should not use this product'. It is alarming that something we are being asked to consume as a healthy food is actually carrying a health warning. Yes, those are alarm bells you can hear.

The ingredients in *Flora pro-activ* are listed as: water, vegetable oils (including sunflower oil), plant sterol esters (12.5%), modified tapioca starch, salt (1.0%), buttermilk, emulsifiers: mono- and di-glycerides of fatty acids, sunflower lecithin, preservative: potassium sorbate, citric acid, vitamin E, flavouring, vitamin B6, folic acid, colour: beta-carotene, vitamins A, D and B12.

Not much to worry about there, you might think. Well, think again.

The first two ingredients, water and vegetable oils, form the essence of most margarines, emulsified together to form a paste. Some of the other ingredients are there to persuade you that this factory product is as good as butter. It isn't. Butter forms naturally from the churning of cream; modern spreads are formed unnaturally with the use of very sophisticated factory equipment and the expertise of white-coated technicians in chemical laboratories. Given these two options for a moment, it is not difficult to understand that the latter is hardly as 'healthy' as the makers claim.

Telling it like it is:

"I prefer butter to margarine, because I trust cows more than I trust chemists."

Joan Dye Gussow

[seen in The Kings Arms in Tedburn St Mary, Devon, where the walls are decorated with quotes about food]

Reluctant to dispute the pronouncements of such a large organisation as Unilever, you might say that there can't be any harm in a bit of vegetable oil, and anyway it's polyunsaturated, so it must be good for you. Wrong again. The list of ingredients states that this brand of Flora contains 'vegetable oils, including sunflower oil'. This suggests that it contains a mix of different oils. Such a mix can change from batch to batch depending on the market price of the various oils, so there will be no guarantee as to exactly what is in the batch that you have just bought. Before being used in Flora, of course, it will be processed to de-odorise it, remove its colour and generally neutralise it, so that any given batch of oil can fit a pre-determined profile before being mixed with the other ingredients.

The lack of guarantee extends to the presence of GM oils. Unless the information on the pack states quite clearly that oils listed in the ingredients are GM-free, then it is not guaranteed. Also, most of them, including the sunflower oil, will be high in Omega-6 fatty acids. Over-consumption of Omega-6 has been linked to cancer, immune system damage and heart disease. So, what about the question of polyunsaturated oils? They are good for us, we are told, but is this really true? According to certain experts on fats, Mary Enig and Sally Fallon for example, polyunsaturated oils are unstable and should never be heated, because they oxidise, rendering them potentially carcinogenic. The oils in this kind of spread have of course been heated during the process of manufacture, so some damage has already been done.

Omega-6 rarely gets a mention these days, because Omega-3 has been hyped up so extensively that it has practically achieved superfood status. But we should be aware of the relationship between these two. In a genuinely natural diet, Omega-3 and Omega-6, are described as essential fatty acids, because the body needs them but cannot make them, so they must be taken in with food. They will be present in a balance of roughly 2:1, Omega-6 to Omega-3, but this is not the case with processed foods, where the balance can be altered by anything up to 20:1 in favour of Omega-6. The benefits of Omega-3 are built up by marketing hype in such a way as to ignore Omega-6, because the products of the modern food industry that contain Omega-3 often contain unnaturally high proportions of Omega-6, and no company wants to admit to this harmful 20:1 imbalance. Such reticence manifests itself in other ways. For instance, our modern food industry is reluctant to tell us that some of the best sources of Omega-3 are eggs, milk, butter and cheese, with the caveat that all these should be from pasture-fed sources, including the eggs. There is no financial benefit to the industry to point us in the direction of these natural foods.

Returning to our ingredients list for *Flora pro-activ*, we see mono- and di-glycerides of fatty acids, described as emulsifiers. This type of emulsifier is also known as a permitted additive under EU legislation, and is listed as E471. E-numbers have become a sensitive issue of late, so it comes as no surprise that the description of this particular emulsifier comes without its corresponding E-number in the ingredients list. What is its purpose? Its job is to hold together the unstable and unnatural mixture of oil and water. In another guise, it is also used in junk foods to stop them from getting stale. But no one in the industry is willingly going to tell you that either.

So, now that we have an emulsifier to hold together our water and oil, we need another substance to thicken it up a bit so that we can spread it on our toast and say to ourselves, "I can't believe it's not butter!" Enter modified tapioca starch. Now, anyone of a certain age will see the word 'tapioca' and immediately be overcome by a wave of nausea as they conjure up pictures of school dinners. This kind of tapioca is worse than that. Note the word 'modified'. An innocent little word that you might easily overlook, but what it means in this context is that starch based on tapioca has been physically or chemically changed to suit the purpose required of it. As much at home in adhesives and explosives as it is in margarine spreads, this modified tapioca starch is not a substance found in nature. It adds no nutritional value and there is no information about any possible effects it might have on our health.

Even with all this going on in our emulsified oil and water concoction, the taste would be pretty uninteresting, but this is easily remedied by adding some flavouring. In any modern foodstuff, something described as a 'flavouring' is the product of a laboratory. Flavourings are no more than synthetic oil-based chemicals. Effectively, they are perfumes, and the ones you find in products such as Flora are not very different from the stuff you find in a bottle of Calvin Klein deodorant. Many are sources of neurotoxins, carcinogens and allergens.

However, it is still technically a free country, so the choice is yours. What would you prefer to spread on your bread, a commercially produced spread like Flora, or naturally produced butter? Hands up those who said butter . . .

Okay, this is where it gets even more interesting. Butter is the right choice but, in this crazy, mixed-up, commercially exploited world in which we live, there is butter and butter. Some butter is produced in a factory, whilst other butter is traditionally churned and comes from the milk of small-scale pasture-fed herds. Although you might be forgiven for thinking that this information could so easily precipitate a fit of depression, it can in fact be quite liberating, because it is confirming all our innate suspicions that 'natural is best.' Thus, the closer a food is to its natural state, the more likely it is to be nutritious.

Factory-made butter is never going to be as good as traditionally churned farmhouse butter, simply because it is made in a factory. End of argument, really. Factory production demands automation, standardisation of product and a constant year-round supply of raw materials in sufficient quantities to keep the factory operating at optimum efficiency. However, this is food we are talking about, and I personally find it distressing to think that it comes from a factory. 'Food' and 'factory' should be mutually exclusive ideas because, by seeking to optimise factory efficiency, the food itself is inevitably compromised. To produce butter in a factory requires a constant flow of cream which will more than likely be obtained from dairy cows that have been burdened with the task of giving up impossibly high yields of milk, brought on by a diet unnaturally high in proteins. In some of the more advanced dairy herds, the natural diet of these herbivores, i.e. fresh grass, dried hay or silage, is practically non-existent. The cows chomp their way through feedstuffs that look like minced doormats and are alien to their systems, simply designed to turn them into living milk machines.

I am sure I can say without fear of contradiction that it is difficult to find food today that has not been adulterated or compromised in some way. The example above, of Flora versus butter, and factory butter *versus* real butter, serves to illustrate just *how* difficult. What it also shows is how simple life would be if we were all able to eat a natural, healthy diet. The good news is that it is still just possible to do that, even though varying degrees of effort are required to achieve this ideal. Eating healthily is relatively easy, despite all the obstacles that have been put in our way.

Defining, and then locating, what is really healthy is where the hard work can be, because the healthiest food is the food you can grow yourself, and most of us do not have our own smallholding. Many of us do not even have what you might call a garden. However, it is surprising what can be grown in a very small space. The concept of growing herbs on a windowsill has become a bit of a symbol of the grow-your-own movement, but a little inventiveness goes a long way, and it is not difficult to get beyond the windowsill. Just for instance, a hanging basket full of cherry tomatoes, a pot or a box planter of dwarf beans on your balcony, or even a bag growing potatoes outside your back door are easy enough to arrange. Driving through Brighton one day, on the way to see my son who lived in Hove at the time, I spotted the marvellous sight of a row of terracotta pots full of runner beans growing on a home made trellis up a set of steps leading to a front door in a terrace of houses.

For the aspiring small-space gardener, there are many books out there that could be considered motivational, amongst which are *Urban Eden* by James Caplin and *Really Small Gardens* by Jill Billington. All that is required to get this kind of project started is the desire to have a go. An even easier start to growing your own is producing your own sprouted seeds – something that can be done even before investing in a hanging basket and some tomato plants. Absolutely bursting with vitality, some would say that sprouted seeds are the ultimate health food. It certainly makes perfect sense to say that a seed which has just germinated is full of life, and of course these sprouted seeds are generally eaten raw in salads, so all that vitality is retained. They are a hugely healthy boost in the early months of the year, in the doldrums between the last of the winter veg and the first of the spring greens, and you can chomp away on your sprouted bean salads while you are waiting for your tomato plants to bear fruit.

Sprouting your own salad seeds

There is really no trick to this. All you need is a good sprouter that will allow your seeds to drain effectively and allow air to circulate. A search for 'seed sprouters' on the internet will throw up a wonderful choice of sprouters to get you started. All you need after that is the seeds. Sally and I favour sunflower, chickpeas, mung beans, buckwheat and hemp, though the last two can be a bit of an acquired taste.

They all behave slightly differently and have varying germination rates, so treat each type separately, whilst following the same basic principles. Soak them until they swell, which could be anything from a couple of hours in the case of buckwheat to 24 hours in the case of hemp. Then drain them and rinse them well. Put them in the sprouter and set them on a windowsill to do their thing. Once a day rinse them again and shake off the surplus water. They will be ready to eat once they begin to sprout.

Some seeds will become bitter if you leave them for more than two or three days before consuming them, but their germination process can be suspended for a short time by putting them in the fridge once they have reached optimum growth.

They are wonderful in salads and, in April and May, when wild plants begin to grow again, they go really well mixed with leaves such as wild garlic, hedge mustard and new hawthorn leaves (pick them while they are still bright green). Sounds wacky, but this kind of salad is brilliant with a home made salad dressing.

We have a friend, Neville, who made some decisions about growing his own produce a while ago. What he did would today be called guerrilla gardening, but at the time it just seemed like a good idea. Neville lives in Guildford, in a small development of '50s flats. One day, on a walk around the estate, he was struck by how much land there was behind a block of garages. Knee-high in nettles and weeds, this plot seemed to Neville to be going to waste. Clearing the nettles and digging up the ground weeds, he realised the soil was good – but filled with the debris left behind by the original builders. Many hours of work ensued as Neville emptied the plot of broken bricks, rubble, old bits of steel girder and other junk.

Finally the plot was ready for cultivation. Neville had produced a garden area about the size of a large bedroom, but with the advantage of having a perimeter wall that enabled him to 'go vertical,' planting runner beans, tomatoes and cucumbers to grow up the walls. Since then, he has also established another smaller plot in the vicinity, where he is growing potatoes in pots, onions, shallots, garlic and more tomatoes. In all, his guerrilla garden, in addition to those vegetables already mentioned, provides him with lettuce, radish, carrots, mini turnips, beetroot, peppers (sweet and hot), peas, savoy cabbage and squash. He also grows basil, mint, sage, marjoram, oregano, rosemary, chives and a bay tree in a container, plus soft fruits such as loganberries and blackberries (against the garage wall) and some melons.

The amount of produce that this new garden actually produces is too much for Neville and his wife, Nina, so Neville has taken to distributing the surplus amongst the little old ladies who live in some of the other flats. Needless to say, Neville has become very popular. To quote from the man himself, "This small plot has given me a great deal of satisfaction, regular exercise (of which my doctor approves), and the benefit of being able to eat fresh produce of known provenance. But there is a greater benefit too, and that is the unquantifiable human element, the actual personal satisfaction of growing your own vegetables to cook and eat at home, and to share with others."

All in all, an extremely good result for such a compact plot. We are so impressed with what he has done here that we have decided to call this kind of enterprising activity 'doing a Nev'. I hope he doesn't mind.

Healthy food is around, but it is so often obscured and difficult to see. However, adhering to a few basic rules and asking a few simple questions will help us enormously in trying to identify those naturally healthy foods around us. Probably the most important question is, "Where has this come from?" In a world fallen from grace, we are faced with a mind-boggling display of so-called foods that are now available to us in our supermarkets. Asking this question will, at the very least, help to establish the length of the chain between you and the original producer. Ideally, of course, the chain should have no links in it at all, thus enabling you to put the question directly to the producer, grower or farmer. The more links you add, the more middlemen become involved and the less likely you are to get a meaningful answer. It will soon become clear to you that most of what is available in a standard supermarket has far too many links and is clearly a long way from natural. You will see that much of it amounts to no more than brand-name factory products vying for shelf space through slick advertising campaigns, of which the Flora marketing machine demonstrates a very efficient example.

To eat healthily, we ultimately need to shun the supermarket, although in the short term it is possible to limit what is bought there to foods that are at least not processed. Some 'foods' have become so much part of our everyday lives that it is difficult to see them as processed, but they most certainly are. These include of course such proprietary branded cereals as Cornflakes, Shredded Wheat or even Weetabix. Despite the 'whole grain' advertising approach, even the more robust branded cereals are processed and nutritionally degraded.

If at all possible, we shouldn't buy anything that is not organic, and we should be aware that 'organic' is a term open to abuse. It is a starting point, a rock to which we can cling in the swirling currents of disinformation. The aim is to buy the best that can be found. For example, we should choose organic, non-homogenised whole milk and wholemeal or rye bread, whose ingredients do not include dubious additives, such as flour improvers, emulsifiers or preservatives. Look for bread baked by small independents, such as The Village Bakery. As a rule of thumb with all packaged foodstuffs, don't touch anything which contains ingredients you cannot pronounce. Act like our ancient ancestors and develop an instinct for food. The instinct is still there – it has just been suppressed. It will reappear if called upon.

There is no magic to this. All you need is a clear understanding of what 'processed' food is, and then you need a strategy for avoiding it and replacing it with real food, in other words, food that is fresh, natural, unadulterated and therefore, by definition, healthy. This is not an exhortation to take up yet another faddy 'health' diet. Neither Sally nor I believe in diets, understanding that enjoyment of food is essential to our wellbeing. So this is not an exercise in cutting out all those irresistible treats that we all enjoy. We should have treats, but by implication, a treat is not an everyday food item.

Eating healthily does not mean that you can never again eat chocolate or crisps or burgers, but it does mean that you should look upon these indulgences as relatively infrequent treats, in which case your body systems will be able to deal with them. Also, take care to buy the best you can find. This lessens the burden on the immune system and increases the enjoyment. Buy the best chocolate you can find, for example, Divine, Plamil or Montezuma, the best hand made crisps, e.g. Tyrells, and the best burgers. With the latter, it is wise to avoid anything from any of the global fast-food chains, because of the contamination of the meat with antibiotic growth hormones and toxic residues from the protein-based animal feeds that prevail in this industry. Better to buy a burger from the local butcher who buys his meat from the local farm or, as you may find this difficult, just make your own at home from steak mince that you have bought from a butcher you know personally (or a reputable mail order company) and who is happy to answer your questions on provenance.

The best home made burgers . . .

Here is a recipe for kotelety taught to me by my Polish mother, and it makes the best burgers ever.

You will need a pound of minced beef, an onion, some butter, an egg, some sea salt and freshly ground black pepper for seasoning and some olive oil to fry the burgers. I must stress that all these ingredients should be organic. Buy them direct from the producer where you can and the rest from an independent wholefood shop.

Melt a knob of butter in a pan. Finely chop the onion and sauté it gently in the butter until wilted and beginning to turn golden brown. Put the mince in a big bowl, add the sautéed onion, the raw egg and season the mix with salt and pepper. Mix thoroughly. You can use a wooden spoon, but I find it is far more successful if you mix it by hand. It seems to blend much more thoroughly – and it really puts you in touch with your food!

Once it is thoroughly mixed, divide the mixture into whatever portions you want. For example, you can split it into four quarter-pounders or six to eight smaller burgers. Fry gently in the heated oil about two minutes each side, giving it a little longer if you want them cooked right through.

You can eat these as they are, served with vegetables, or you can let them go cold and serve them as part of a cold platter, or you can indeed eat them as a burger, in which case, it's great fun to make your own bread rolls. Not just good fun, but a chance to make them with good organic ingredients [see Chapter 10 for a recipe]. And, if you have children, get them involved – let them into the secrets of making their own burgers. Pizzas could be next . . .

When eyes are open and awareness raised, it is surprising how many new sources of food will come to mind. This gives us all a chance to change our shopping patterns without too much disruption. For instance, if you know there is a Farmer's Market in town next week, go to it. Putting in the effort to buy directly from the producer is well worth it. Believe in your goal without making it unattainable. If you change at your own pace, you will be impressed by how easily change will happen. All that is really required as a catalyst is the desire to change. After that, one step at a time and a steady pace will take you to your destination. Keep your mind on the four criteria – fresh, seasonal, local and unadulterated – and try to judge every purchase against them. Before you know it, you will have moved away from old habits. This rejuvenating process will see you enjoying a completely different shopping experience, really taking charge of your food once again and, best of all, eating healthily.

Chapter Three

Eat . . . seasonally

Emerging from the swirling mists of food industry spin to reach the high ground of common sense is worth the climb. It is exhilarating to look down on the clouded vista below and know that, from this vantage point, it is possible to see clearly all around and to take in the extent of the haze below us. Fog-bound gloom gives way to brilliant sunshine. The obfuscatory tactics of profit-motivated companies hold no power to deceive in the bright light of understanding.

We are so easily persuaded by glib marketeers to think in a particular, even peculiar, way. Marketing experts apply sophisticated psychology to gnaw away at our neuroses and tip the scales towards our fears, firstly creating a problem that we didn't know we had and then offering a solution that we didn't know we needed. Nowhere is this more intensely applied than in the food and health industry. It is hard to slip off the shackles of fear imposed by the new food gurus but, once we do, the freedom can be euphoric. Foods that we once faced with, at best, mistrust and at worst, repulsion, can again be enjoyed as our forebears enjoyed them.

Taking the time to seek out natural nutritious fare increases our enjoyment of food, changing it from an exercise in fear-driven calorie counting paranoia, or just another routine fuel stop, into the holistic experience it should be. A comprehension of the vital need we all have for real nutrition inspires in us a new and keen interest in what our food is and where it comes from. Enjoying our food creates a different kind of hunger – a hunger for knowledge. We simply need to know more about what we eat, not only about its provenance but also about how it actually grows, where it grows, when it is ready to eat and how best to prepare it for the table.

We discover an interest in gardening that maybe we didn't know we possessed, and thus learn more about the delights, surprises and even disappointments of seasonal produce. The challenges of actually producing food for the table become all too apparent when we go out into the garden one morning and find that the slugs have chewed off the tops of all the bean seedlings. Yet such frustrating irritations are more than compensated for when finally one is able to harvest vegetables and fruit in abundance. And how else can we experience such delights as the wonderful taste of thinnings from the onion bed, or the leaves of young beet plants, without growing them ourselves? Furthermore, there is great comfort in understanding that everything has a season, not just asparagus, and it brings our culinary inventiveness to the fore. Cooking takes on a whole new meaning. It is no longer something that is performed for us as some kind of entertainment by so-called celebrity chefs. It begins to look more like an innate skill that has lain in dormant anticipation of that moment when we come into the kitchen with a basket full of freshly picked vegetables and decide spontaneously what to do with them.

Though to some this may sound a bit starry-eyed, it is no more than my own experience of what it is like to see the picture. In the mid-nineties, a book was published called *Magic Eye*, which became very popular for a while. It consisted of a number of pages of what looked like nothing more than squiggles of colourful patterns. However, looked at in a certain way, an unexpected and remarkably clear 3-D image would emerge from each page. I am reminded of this book when I think of what has happened to my own perception of food.

Once the hidden picture is seen, it is impossible to view the overall image without knowing that there is something more meaningful within it. Thus our attitude to food changes. The graven images of convenience, cheapness and year-round abundance imposed upon us by the high priests of our supermarket deism are toppled by Zen and the Art of Real Food. False gods all, we soon see that there is nothing *convenient* about shopping in a warehouse crammed with an endless array of factory products, nothing *cheap* about buying nutritionally empty foodstuffs and nothing desirable about *year-round abundance* when the choice on display is the same, week in, week out, month after month, year after year. Where is the fun, the stimulation and excitement in having the same selection of fruit and vegetables every month of every year? As if this is not bad enough, the shape, size and colour spectrum of the standard supermarket range do not change either.

Seasonality is what defines our food, and any alternative to this basic concept is a distortion where quantity prevails over quality, and uniformity over diversity. The supermarket claims dominion over seasonality, but it can do that only by freighting in fruit and vegetables from around the world to maintain the lie that it is natural to eat all things all year round. It is not natural, neither is it particularly desirable. To live with the false notion that we can and should be able to eat what we like when we like is to reduce our relationship with food to that of a kid in a sweetshop. It has no more meaning than that. When we are motivated by quality, however, we soon realise that the excellence we seek comes only from really fresh food – the kind of food that comes into season in our own local area and is available to us as it reaches its peak of ripeness.

In the real world, the seasons define life. Not just fruit and vegetables, but the whole of the life force that makes our tiny planet unique within the known cosmos. To begin to perceive this is empowering. To sense the elemental spirit of the Earth re-awaken in spring after the slumber of winter is a deeply moving, if not humbling, experience. It reconnects us. We are an inextricable part of that life force, and tuning into it is a heady moment that heightens our perception of what is truly important. Walking around our garden in

April, Sally and I are moved by the vital force of Nature re-emerging each spring. We see how the different elements of nature work in harmony, with certain early flowers appearing just at the time that bumble bee queens emerge from hibernation to seek new locations to start the next colony. The flowers depend on the bees for pollination, and the bees depend on the flowers for food. We depend on the bees pollinating the flowers, so that we can have fruit and vegetables to eat in the summer. Knowing that all living things, even we humans, are governed by the seasonal cycle, is liberating. It brings with it a profound clarity of the significance of seasonal food.

An autumn celebration . . . with Sally's plum upside down cake

Once the autumn fruits start to appear, what a good excuse to make comforting puddings like this one. English plums can be found in the farm shops and farmers markets from July through to early October but it is highly unlikely that any of the wonderful varieties that are grown in this country will be found in the supermarkets.

The choice they so boldly claim to give their customers does not exist when it comes to plums. Instead it seems they are prepared to stock only the outrageously colourful and tasteless varieties from Europe and South America, because they are easier to handle, have a good shelf life and travel well.

Unfortunately many of our old orchards have been grubbed up for the sake of growing wheat and other cash crops, but if you are lucky enough to have a traditional orchard near you then seek out the varieties that are local to your area. You might find Marjorie's Seedlings, Blue Tit, Czar, Excalibur or Early Rivers. The ubiquitous but much loved Victoria plum works very well in this recipe but you could try using a mixture of varieties creating different shapes and colours for an added wow. I try to use rapadura sugar (dehydrated sugar cane) wherever I think it appropriate, simply because it is better for you. It also gives cakes a darker, richer look as well as adding a hint of toffee to the taste. If you can't find rapadura in your local whole food shop you could substitute light muscovado.

Plum upside down pudding cake

It is taken as read that all ingredients are the best you can find. You will need a deep 9" cake tin with a fixed base and buttered.

For the bottom layer
Approximately 700g of plums
(you may need less but certainly not more)
50g rapadura sugar
25g organic unsalted butter
Melt the rapadura with the butter and then spread the mixture over the bottom of the tin. Stone the plums, trying to keep them whole, and tightly pack them on top of the butter and sugar mixture - there shouldn't be any gaps between them.

Preheat the oven to 180°C

Cake mixture

110g softened organic unsalted butter
110g organic self-raising flour (I use 50% white and 50% wholewheat)
25g ground almonds
½ teaspoon baking powder
3 large organic eggs
Few drops of almond essence
80g rapadura sugar

Sift the flour, baking powder and ground almonds together and set aside. Lightly whisk the eggs with one or two drops of the almond essence. Beat the butter and rapadura sugar together until very soft then as you continue to mix, tip in one third of the flour and then one third of the eggs. Repeat until all the ingredients have been incorporated and you have a soft dropping consistency.

Spoon the mixture over the plums making sure you completely cover them. Put the tin in the oven for about 45 minutes until the cake has shrunk away from the sides of the tin and the top is golden brown. Remove from the oven and leave to cool for 10 minutes. Take a spatula and run the blade around the edge of the tin, take a shallow dish or plate and place it over the top of the cake tin. Turn the whole ensemble upside down and place the plate on the work surface. Very carefully lift off the cake tin using the spatula to remove any fruit or cake that is sticking to the tin.

My preference is to serve this warm and, although custard is possibly the traditional accompaniment, I do like thick jersey cream with a pudding of this sort.

Though we do grow a reasonable selection of fruit and vegetables at home, Sally and I get a good proportion of what we need from Martin and Rachel Soble at Whitethorn Farm, an organic market garden less than two miles away. It cannot be denied that having a source of organic produce so close to us is a boon, but it wasn't always this easy. Five years ago, the land lay quietly dormant as set-aside, having in the past been subjected to the rigours of chemically supported intensive wheat and potato production. It may well have gone that way again, but it is a difficult patch of land for intensive cultivation, though ideal for Martin and Rachel. So these 45 acres were saved from chemically induced death by someone who had an idea that he would like to grow organic fruit and vegetables.

Martin and Rachel used to live in Hampshire, doing what millions of others do, jogging ceaselessly on society's hamster cage treadmill. With family connections in farming and gardening, however, they at least kept in touch with nature by growing their own vegetables at home and seeing life differently from many of their contemporaries. Finally, disenchanted with modern consumerism, discussions took place and some kind of change became inevitable. As with all such changes in direction, the new way forward was not completely clear, but what was certain was that some good land was required on which to establish, at the very least, an orchard growing a range of old English apple varieties.

The forty-five acres that became Whitethorn Farm (aka Carey Organic) looked ideal, but no house was for sale with the land. Renting a holiday home in the village, they sought temporary planning permission for a dwelling on the site, finally spending a short time in a caravan with their two young children whilst organising the construction of the log cabin which became their new home. Meanwhile, a 23-acre orchard of apples, pears, plums, cherries and cider apples was established with the planting of four thousand trees in March 2005. Since then, soft fruit, such as raspberries, gooseberries, strawberries and currants of various hue have extended the range on offer to their customers. Vegetables soon followed and gradually, as Martin and Rachel established themselves and gained certified organic status, our own need to buy fruit and vegetables from other sources was somewhat reduced.

These two hard-working individuals are not living the dream, in the popular sense of the phrase. They are not emulating the accepted stereotype of indulging in the good life. What they have taken on is arguably harder than the work they left. At times it just looks like a gruelling 7-day-a-week schedule involving much outside work that has to be done however foul the weather might be. Since establishing Whitethorn Farm four years ago, they rear pigs too, as well as maintaining a flock of hens to provide a supply of eggs, and all these animals have to be fed every day. The vagaries of the weather, especially in these newly unsettled climatic times, can upset animals, ruin crops and wipe out profits. To maximise profitability, Martin was at one time advised to cover the whole of his acreage in polytunnels to grow soft fruit for the supermarkets. But this was never an option, and not what he and Rachel had set out to do, which was to grow a rich variety of produce to supply local customers all year round.

For Martin and Rachel, this move represents a real change of lifestyle. By renouncing profligate consumerism in favour of a life in which the core human values of cooperation, community and family still apply, they have opted for the chance of bringing up their children in a better environment, in every sense of the word. They have of course given up one demanding schedule of work for another, but now all choices and decisions are their own. No longer selling their time to the highest bidder, they have found this concept has far less relevance when working for themselves. They now enjoy a life of more meaning and greater satisfaction, creating a truly local enterprise, sharing skills, resources and ideas with others in the immediate locality and selling most of their produce within a very small radius.

Sally and I now find it difficult to remember 'life before Whitethorn Farm.' We certainly bought our fruit and vegetables locally, but it was not always direct from the producer. Effectively, we were making the best of what we had, whilst trying to source all our fresh produce from within a 10-mile radius. To have Martin and Rachel on our doorstep is inestimably satisfying. To know that we can go down there and buy vegetables which have just been pulled from the ground is very nearly as rewarding as growing them ourselves. In fact, on those occasions when Martin or Rachel are not around, I have been known to pick my own and just leave them a note to tell them what I've had – working on trust is so civilised. The food we produce at Aspen House has to comply with our own ideal of 'simple but effective,' and that is the way it has been since we opened for business. Having Whitethorn Farm so close, however, has elevated our thinking to a new level. We no longer think, "We'll do this simple dish for our guests tonight – let's go out and buy the ingredients." Now our advance meal planning usually starts with the phrase, "I wonder what they've got down at Whitethorn?"

Without conscious effort, just through having such wonderful fresh produce available nearby, we have come to think both 'locally' and 'seasonally.' Most particularly, it is the seasonal aspect of what takes place at Whitethorn that has had the most positive effect on us. Though we have always had an awareness of seasonality, to be close to a farm where fruit and vegetables are grown reinforces that understanding. Talking to someone who grows fruit and vegetables commercially even helps to redefine 'seasonality' for us. As Martin points out, the seasons simply fit together neatly, creating an almost continuous stream of produce in a never ending cycle, leaving only the few weeks around May when supply becomes a little sporadic. When we talk to Martin or Rachel about which varieties of which crop come into prime condition as the year unfolds, and how changes in the weather affect the crop, positively or negatively, the holistic experience of food takes on a new meaning. It is at times like these that I begin to comprehend what Fukuoka was saying about eating naturally. Eating what is available in any given season has unexpectedly lifted our spirits and removed from us the burden of how to be innovative in the kitchen when faced with the supermarket cornucopia of permanent global summertime.

Recipe for success . . .

"You don't have to cook fancy or complicated masterpieces –
just good food from fresh ingredients."
Julia Child (1912 – 2004)

There are those who wonder why we should bother with seasonality, a notion that they see as quaint, outdated and nostalgic. They would ask what is the point in getting all dewy-eyed about it when it appears to them to be nothing more than a whimsical ideal.

The point is that we stand at a T-junction in the history of our species. We have two simple choices, two directions in which to go. One is to follow the course set out for us since the inception of chemical farming, and the other is to make our peace with Nature. If we take the first direction, the way is clearly marked by the flag wavers of industrial agriculture, who march down the road amid much hullabaloo chanting the mantra, "We must feed the world, we must feed the world." The other direction is much quieter. Here we have no glitz, no glamour – just some calm clear-thinking people who say, "We can feed the world, but we can do that only by teaching the world to feed itself."

Think about what this choice means. Industrial farming, and the globalised food industry that feeds off it, is killing us. It might be killing the planet too, but I suspect that the planet will recover, whereas we might not. With industrial farming comes mechanisation, unmitigated use of toxic chemicals, the slow death of our soils and the poisoning of our rivers and aquifers. It has taken from us our connection with Nature, our instinctive relationship with food and our ability to think for ourselves. It has virtually destroyed whatever food culture and culinary heritage we ever had. We have forgotten how to grow, how to cook and how to eat, and our early warning system for detecting harmful ingredients has withered into uselessness, killed by the very toxins we are no longer able to detect.

Standing at our T-junction, it is evident that we can no longer follow this course of action, this disastrous model for unlimited growth that has made an enemy of Nature whilst simultaneously undermining our own social structures. The only other choice now open to us is in the opposite direction. We must be reconciled with Nature and recognise that we are inextricably linked with all natural systems. What better place to start than with seasonal food?

Before the industrialisation of agriculture, there was a time when we were comfortably in tune with the seasons. It was important to us to know when to plant different crops, when to harvest them and how to preserve and store any surplus during the lean winter months. Though it was necessary to our survival to be possessed of such knowledge, there was a huge pay-off in the fact that we were eating food at its best, as well as maximising nutrition in the abundant seasons to give us a good chance of getting through the lean times. Seasonal awareness encompassed knowledge of Nature's wild larder as well as our own home-grown foods, adding to what was available for sustenance.

Today, the majority of us have cut ourselves off from this awareness, but for a country boy like me the memory of it is sharp. My father was a seasonal gardener, and his efforts kept our family in vegetables throughout the year. Even during the winter months, with the vegetable patch under an eiderdown of snow, the garden provided us with cabbages, Brussels sprouts, leeks, parsnips and swedes. Some might scorn these humble roots and staid brassicas but, taken straight from the garden to the kitchen, they were positively jumping with nutrition. My father's horticultural skills were learned from his father before him – Grandpa's garden too was an exercise in self-sufficiency. Many miles from the nearest shop, and without the convenience of a car, self-sufficiency was vital to the family's wellbeing.

As a boy on Grandpa's farm, I experienced the fascination of watching the process of growth in the vegetable garden. I was amazed by the speed with which vegetables sprang from nothing but a few delicate shoots in the brown earth to a profusion of flowers and foliage. In what seemed like only a few weeks, vegetables were ready for digging up, pulling or cutting. As the snows of winter melted into spring, new life began to push through ground still twinkling with early morning frost. Even as the tired remnants of snow-capped Brussels sprouts bowed under the weight of their iced leaves, the dark soil over the rhubarb corms would split to reveal a tightly furled shiny leaf.

This was the signal for Grandpa to bring out a couple of old coal scuttles – the tall ones with the two handles on the side – to put over the burgeoning crowns. The scuttles were no longer fit for the purpose of carrying coal, as the bottoms had rusted out, but they were perfect for forcing rhubarb. As the leaves struggled upwards towards the light, the stems turned red in the gloom of the metal tubes. By the time the leaves had reached the daylight through the upturned rusty scuttles, the stems inside were ready to be snapped out of their horseshoe-shaped moorings, their bulbous white ends often tinted with a delicate pink. Taken into the kitchen for Granny to transform them into a rhubarb pie for the dinner table, these crimson stems really did signify the start of the new season in the garden, overlapping with the last of the leeks and parsnips from the grey days of winter.

As the year rolled out, so the varieties of vegetables changed, each one marking another click on the wheel of this horticultural clock. By the time the rhubarb had outgrown the confines of its metal prison and had been left to mature more naturally, producing green stems flecked with red, thinnings from the rows of radishes, cloched lettuce and early carrots were being picked for the kitchen. Waiting for early new potatoes felt like an eternity, yet in reality no more than a couple of months from planting out. To taste that first crop, cooked in minted water and brought to the table tossed in butter and fresh parsley was an experience, the memory of which is as strong today as it ever was. Every year, I try to recreate it at my own table, using old-fashioned garden mint and parsley straight from the garden just as Granny did. Occasionally, I get it right, and the taste is the key that opens up a door to my memory. A clear panorama of childhood experiences is glimpsed in that instant. It is an indication of the importance of food that one simple taste from the past will evoke strong and vivid memories of life at that time.

On Grandpa's farm, as well as on those of his neighbours, new life was not restricted to the vegetable plot, but came in the shape of lambs, calves and piglets, to say nothing of the little garden birds, busy in the trees and hedgerows. Grass in the meadows grew green, glossy and lush, whilst Jack-by-the-Hedge clustered around the perimeters and along the hedgerows, vying for space with stinging nettles and a dozen other edible wild plants. In the woods, the wild garlic would appear in great green swathes, splashed with delicate heads of white flowers, like sparkling tiny starbursts. Granny never had the inclination to gather such delicacies for the table, but, the old gamekeeper's wife down the lane, blessed with the wonderfully rustic name of Grizzel Grice, would happily cook them up as 'greens'. She said they went well with her squirrel pie.

Spring sighed into summer and my childhood world basked in its warmth. Translucent frail beech leaves thickened and darkened, throwing a dappled shade over the spinney below the farm, keeping the heat off the badger setts and allowing the delicate white anemones to bloom in profusion, scattered amongst the tree roots as if broadcast by an unseen hand. Summer had a kind of laziness to it, a sort of drowsy contentment, the air filled with dandelion seed heads parachuting over the garden hedge. The buzz of the bumble bee and the flicker of butterflies eased us through our time of plenty. Vegetables and fruit were abundant by the time of the school summer holidays, with strawberries for tea, or gooseberry crumble. Strawberries gave way to currants and raspberries, and they in turn heralded the first plums and early apples. Each fruit season culminated in a glut, and Granny would be busy bottling some fruit and making some into jam. As the days shortened and the cornfields turned a dull yellow, big Bramleys would ripen in the orchard, bending the branches of the trees behind Grandpa's summerhouse, its edges softened by long grass and brambles beneath the ancient gnarled boughs of this quiet corner of the farm.

Sally's summer fruit jam

We are lucky enough to have Carey Organic less than two miles down the road, as well as Treberva Fruit Farm three miles in the opposite direction. As the spring warms into summer, fruit comes into season, ripening all at once and producing a glut. For me this is a perfect opportunity to take advantage of this time of plenty to do something that was commonplace only a generation ago. As the summer progresses, different fruits come into their own, giving us all the chance to make either a single variety jam or a mixed summer fruit jam with loganberries, raspberries, strawberries and blackcurrants. The basic jam recipe calls for 1lb of fruit, but it is easy enough to multiply the quantities. I am not going to quote a set amount of sugar, because I am a great believer in starting with the minimum and then tasting as I go. The tradition is 1lb of sugar to 1lb of fruit but, by lowering the sugar content, the fruity flavour of the jam is much more intense. There is a chance that you might be reducing the keeping time, but I find that all jams keep well if the rules of clean bottling have been followed. I must add that Rob makes a Polish plum jam, *powidła*, which uses no sugar at all if the plums are really ripe, and it keeps really well. To be on the safe side, just keep jam in the fridge once the jar has been opened.

A number of people I talk to have been put off jam-making because the jam comes out rock hard or too runny, so here's a quick word about setting point. There is really no substitute for visual observation. As the jam reaches setting point, the fruit mixture does not rise as vigorously in the preserving pan, it makes more noise as it boils and large bubbles begin to appear on the surface – I liken this to the mud springs of New Zealand! When I first started making jams, I found I was forever shuffling cold jam-laden saucers in and out of the freezer. Well, there is another way. One day, I decided I would just let the jam go cold in the pan and then check it. That gave me a chance to test it for sweetness (by having a bit on my breakfast toast!) and to add perhaps some agave syrup if I thought it was still a little sharp. If I am happy with the taste and consistency, I merely heat it through thoroughly without further boiling. Once it is reheated in this way, I just bottle it as normal.

Recipe

When mixing fruit to make jam, cook the firmest fruit first, adding the others as you go along. This ensures all the fruit is cooked to the same consistency before adding the sugar, because once sugar is added, the skins will not soften further.

1lb organic summer fruits (not over ripe)
9-10oz white Fairtrade organic sugar (add more if required)
2tbs organic lemon juice

Check fruit is clean and free of bruises, and place in a preserving pan. Gently simmer the fruit as above to ensure that the maximum amount of pectin is released. Once lightly cooked, add sugar and lemon juice, ensuring that the sugar dissolves slowly. Taste as it dissolves and, if not sweet enough, add more, but make sure it is still on the lowest heat. Once you are happy with the taste and all the sugar is dissolved, raise the heat to a rapid boil so that setting point is reached in the shortest time. Pour into hot clean jars and seal with waxed circles immediately. Store in a cool, dark cupboard.

I remember the delight of apple harvesting. With the leaves turning yellow, and the Cox's Orange Pippins flashing their red-striped golden skins, it was time to gather what was left before the frosts bruised them. Out would come the old wooden ladders and willow baskets, and we would systematically go through the orchard gathering the fruit. Space was made on the dusty elm-boarded floor of the apple loft, and Grandpa would spread out pages of newspapers he had been saving for this particular purpose. Checking each apple for bruising or maggots, the sound ones were laid out in rows on the newspaper, Grandpa supervising me to make sure that I didn't leave any apples touching each other. No photographs were ever taken of what was no doubt seen by the elders as a fairly mundane but necessary annual ritual, but I still carry sharp pictures in my head of the shafts of sunlight coming through the window in the roof and washing over the brightly coloured rows of fruit. These would be a welcome addition to our food supply in the winter. In a good year the stocks would just about see us through to the following spring.

Beneath the apple loft was the coal house, where in a dark corner potatoes and carrots were also stored for the winter. The potatoes would have been left dirty but allowed to dry on the ground before putting them into sacks for keeping. The carrots would be stored in a makeshift 'clamp', effectively just a container of dry sandy earth in which the carrots were buried. Parsnips were left in the ground, because it was generally believed that they tasted better after a bit of frost. I have since found out that this is no old wives' tale. Frost helps to turn some of the starches in the parsnip to sugar, thus giving them a sweeter flavour. So in the ground they stayed and were always good to eat right through to about March, when they started to get a bit woody around the core.

On the ground floor of the house, just down the hall from the kitchen, was the pantry. Before the days of refrigeration, this was a vital storage area. Facing north-east, it was a cool space away from direct sunlight. The smell on opening the door was, like Granny's buttered potatoes, one of those evocative bouquets of the past. I find it hard to describe today, but to catch a trace of it again would be to transport me instantly back to the old homestead. It was a combination of cured bacon, butter, milk, cheese and cream, with hints and notes of pies and cakes, all of which somehow seemed to be enhanced by the cold dull white marble on which the various dishes and plates sat. It is now no more than a memory, an aroma of a different time, a different life. Yet it is not the dewy-eyed remembrance of some golden age when 'things were so much better than today.' In many ways, day-to-day existence was harder then. No electricity, mains sewage, running water or central heating meant life was far from the comfort zone it is in our modern age. Waking up on a winter's morning, with the bedroom windows opaque with Paisley-pattern frosted fronds, was no fun at all. Tramping along to the bottom of the garden past the snowy vegetable plot, to sit on a cold board in the privy was not a bundle of laughs either, nor was the back-breaking work of washing clothes in a big copper tub under which a fire had to be lit in order to heat the water.

For all that which we now perceive as hardship, however, it was still a life in which human values and a respect for nature defined a worthwhile existence. To reclaim some of those values would be not just desirable, but essential, and it can be done simply enough just by heeding the seasons once again, for they define the way in which nature works. Every species on the planet except for Man sets its calendar according to the seasons, because the seasons influence when food is plentiful, when it is time for a slowing down of activity to conserve energy and when the time is right for new life to begin. Although today it is somewhat academic to talk about a diet which is exclusively composed of seasonal food, there is an urgent need to reacquaint ourselves with seasonality. At the very least, we should understand the existence of the seasons, because we are then equipped to understand what can easily be grown, reared and consumed in those seasons. This understanding is fundamental to our ability to construct a working model for growing, cooking and eating fresh local produce at its nutritional peak.

Despite the technologists' claims that 'Mother Nature doesn't always know best' and Man is such a superior species that nothing is beyond our capabilities, we are still reminded every day that Nature, not Man, rules the world. A respect for the seasons is a respect for Nature, and a respect for Nature is the first step towards repairing the damage that we have caused in the name of our own self-deluded definition of progress.

A seasonal tale with a dark side

In my last couple of years at school, I used to do summer holiday jobs to gain a modicum of financial independence. We lived two miles from Pershore, on the western edge of the Vale of Evesham market garden heartland, and one summer I worked at Pershore Growers, a wholesale operation.

As each new crop came into season, there was serious competition amongst the growers to be first to offer it for sale. Being first meant being paid a high price. As the season progressed, the price would drop and, in a good season, the abundance of any one crop might mean that some growers ended up ploughing the remainder of it back into the ground, this being a cheaper option than actually harvesting it.

At Pershore Growers itself, the situation was slightly different. What happened there was that the price offered to the growers descended rapidly as the season advanced, but the price at which the crop was sold into the retail trade was kept artificially high. How was this done? Simply by keeping a proportion of the harvest back and not letting it into the retail market, thus ensuring that the wholesale price remained viable.

The day I found out about this was the day I asked the foreman why there were pallets full of cauliflowers rotting at the back of the yard. "Oh, well, we do that to keep the price up, see?" he told me, "We don' want too many of them caulis out there, otherwise we don' make any money."

For me, that was a very early lesson in the workings of the wholesale trade. The grower is the one putting in all the work and bearing most of the risk, whereas the wholesaler is the one who is simply making money out of handling the produce. One extra link in the chain adds one more bit of profit that has to be found between the grower and his customer, and the process takes on a slightly unethical hue, a dark colour which deepens as more links are added to the chain.

Chapter Four

Eat . . . ethically

Around here, where we live in rural Herefordshire, it's the same story every year. The land is being worked to death. In some places there is so little life left in the soil that it simply turns to sand in the heat of summer or into a brown slurry during heavy rain. So much comes off certain fields that the Council has to send out a workforce to remove the sandy sludge from the roads, where it has created a beach landscape in miniature. Yet every year, the same agricultural mistakes that have caused this problem in the first place are made all over again.

As soon as a crop is harvested, be it wheat, maize, rapeseed or potatoes, the land is ploughed, dosed up with chemical fertiliser and sown again with a new crop. The land is exhausted. It sustains no life, other than the chemically supported crops. If a clod is picked up, it can be crumbled to dust in the hand. There is no organic matter in it to hold it together. No worms or insects are evident in this barren earth, and the birds no longer follow the plough, as they used to on my Grandpa's farm. What birds are left, after so many of them have perished eating the toxic seed that falls during harvest time, have given up hope of ever finding anything edible in this dead soil.

Many who visit us here in Herefordshire speak in envious tones of our life in the country, away from the grimness of urban pollution. Their eyes take in the rural vision, with a patchwork of fields stretching away to the foothills of the Welsh mountains, and they marvel at the pastoral scene. We too feel comforted by the beauty of this vista, and we would be the first to agree that the scenery around the Welsh Borders is stunning. But we have reservations about how the land is being farmed. What visitors to Herefordshire cannot 'see' is the industrialisation of those fields and the liberal use of pesticides upon them. They don't see the sinister crop sprayers with their ugly outstretched arms systematically pouring noxious pesticides over growing plants. If they stay with us during harvest time, they will no doubt see the mammoth tractors pulling huge trailers full of potatoes, but they can't see the harmful residues within the flesh of these tubers. They see the combines at work in hedgeless fields, chomping through acres of wheat in just a few short hours, but they don't see that wheat being transported to far-off factories, where it will be turned into white sliced loaves, lifeless white flour, tasteless frozen pizza bases and cheap cakes.

Very few understand that the fields of Herefordshire, or anywhere else in the UK or the rest of the world for that matter, are literally crushed by the wheels of industrialisation. The crops grown on these fields are making no real contribution to feeding anyone. They simply feed the food processing industry. Industrial farming in the UK and the rest of Europe is ecologically destructive, but it is even worse in other parts of the world. In the USA, according to Martin Teitel in his book, *Rain Forest in Your Kitchen*, two thirds of the harvestable cropland is given over to chemically supported monocultures of corn, wheat and soya. Considering that his book was written in 1992 and he was quoting from a report published in 1983, it is a sobering thought that the situation was already that bad nearly thirty years ago. It is worse today. It is all about money, and the precious life of our soil is seemingly squandered for the sake of short-term profits. To brand farming 'a business like any other' is to give birth to this mockery of an agricultural heritage and to condemn the parent culture to death. To run our agriculture as a cost-cutting, profit-maximising factory system has been one of the greatest disasters of the 20th Century. My Grandpa would hardly recognise what is going on today. He would look in horror at the highly mechanised agri-business that has turned our land into commodity-crop prairies, ripping out the hedgerows and the life they contained to create ever bigger fields, and pushing all people off the land except the handful needed to drive the giant tractors and combines.

This is not farming; this is exploitation. What we all like to think of as real farming is something carried out by just a few dedicated people who are proud of their tradition and have no wish to give up without a fight. But it is also a heartbreakingly difficult lifestyle for most of them, because they are under such pressure from the dominant forces of agri-business. They are under constant threat, and many fall victim to these powerful forces each year, as farms go bankrupt or farmers just leave the land because they are exhausted. As life ebbs from our farming tradition, new blood is simply not being transfused quickly enough.

"The cost of a thing is the amount of what I call life which is required to be exchanged for it, immediately or in the long run."
Henry David Thoreau [1817 – 1862]

Imagine this. You have decided to take up farming, in order to opt out of the rat-race. So you sell your house, move to the middle of nowhere and buy yourself some land.

You grow crops, which you need to sell in order to pay for your everyday bills and running costs. However, when it comes to selling them, there is only one buyer willing to purchase what you are growing. He simply tells you what price he is going to pay, take it or leave it. You know it's not as much as you need as it barely covers your costs, but you have no choice, so you capitulate and sell your crop at a loss in the hope that next year someone else will come along.

Next year, it's the same buyer with a different story. He is still willing to buy from you, but at a reduced price compared with the first year. Once again, it is take it or leave it . . .

A nightmare scenario? A non-starter? A business model like this would not make it past even the most adventurous of risk-takers amongst the banks and loan institutions. Any business plan including this sort of suicidal sales concept would be binned without further scrutiny. Yet this is stark reality for tens of thousands of farmers and growers all over the world, from the UK to China and from the USA to Africa, India and Asia. Of course, no one would willingly enter a loss-making enterprise of this nature, so what we find, in the UK certainly, is that those who are locked into such a bleak relationship with ruthless buyers have generally inherited their farms and are trying to continue as their forebears did. Reluctant as they are to trade under such aggressive terms, they do not want to lose their lands, so they are reluctantly putting up with it whilst praying for a positive change in their circumstances. Struggling against overwhelming odds, many do not survive, as the fingernails that kept them clinging to the precipice finally break and send them tumbling to oblivion.

This is farming under global rules. This is also Britain today, where the suicide rate amongst farmers is consistently around twice the national average – a tragic and lonely end to what has become for many of our small-scale farmers a problem with no solution. And every time any one of us goes into a supermarket to shop, we are contributing to that problem. Though we do it unwittingly, we are condoning the kind of cheap-at-any-cost ethos that keeps these global retailers in competition with each other and, in doing so, screws the price paid to suppliers into the ground. The truth is unpalatable, yet the virulent supermarket culture is responsible for the ruthless cut-throat buying that drives farmers to suicide, here in our own home counties just as much as in India, Africa and the rest of the world.

The profits made by the agri-business industrialists, as well as by the food factories and supermarkets they supply, are lauded by a succession of blinkered governments and 'captains of industry' as being good for the national economy. But the economy is a failed model that has achieved little more than to exploit the Earth's resources to create mountains of waste whilst making a tiny handful of individuals exceedingly rich. As for the profits in question, these would not be possible without sales, and those sales come from each one of us. So long as we, the final customers in this chain of exploitation, continue to buy the products churned out by the food factories, so our farmland will continue to be exploited in this way.

When we first opened our doors for business at Aspen House, Sally and I bought from supermarkets every week, falling into the convenience trap as readily as anyone else. Gradually, however, we have come to understand how, in a grotesque mirror image of the natural world, the unnatural world is globally and imperceptibly linked with a web of unnatural systems, of which modern human society is a part. The activities of our species has created a monstrous artificial ecology whose tentacles spread into every part of the planet, distorting, poisoning and killing the natural ecology that it has smothered. Our meat and dairy animals, to say nothing of the food they eat, are now, in part at least, artificial, or not as nature intended. Even wild fish in every ocean of the world swim in waters tainted by Man's activities.

Sally and I have come to see clearly our contribution in all of this, and how the food purchasing decisions we used to make were inextricably bound up with all that takes place in the gigantic global food system. It was hard for us to accept that we were contributing to the problems of land degradation and ecological destruction, but books like *Rain Forest in Your Kitchen* spelled it out for us. Once we understood, we found ourselves unable to shop in a supermarket again. It was as simple as that. Whatever the implications of finding alternative ways of shopping, we were prepared to do that in order to withdraw our custom from those businesses. Our personal stance was that it was ethically wrong to support such destructive systems. Even though seeking an alternative might have cost us some time, and possibly some money, we felt that our continued support of a system that threatens not only our own health but also the life of the planet is morally repugnant.

Slow pot-roasted shoulder of hogget

As an interesting take on the idea of eating ethically, here is a recipe for a dish that has become very popular at Aspen House. Around Easter, with that feeling of spring in the air, many people will turn their thoughts to new season's lamb. There is something iconic about lamb at Easter time, but for Sally and me there is a question mark over the ethics of raising lambs for Easter, because that means they must be born in the cold months of winter in order to make it to the table in time. We are not condemning the custom of lamb at Easter, but we believe that we can suggest something altogether more delicious, and that is hogget – meat from a yearling sheep. Hype and marketing have put lamb at the centre of our attention as the only sheep meat worth eating, as a result of which so many of us miss out on the delights of meat that is a little more mature. You won't find hogget in the supermarket, but you will find it from mail order suppliers like Graig Farm. If you can't find hogget, try mutton, also excellent to eat.

When we talk about hogget or even mutton, the usual reaction is one of prejudice. Received wisdom tells us that mature sheep meat is tough, yet that same wisdom tells us that mature beef is tender. With a similar lack of logic, the other part of the myth is that it is wrong to eat veal, because it comes from a young bullock, but it is okay to eat the meat from a very young sheep.

Sidestepping the argument, but with our eye on the ethics of 'forcing' meat production, we simply serve this slow pot-roasted hogget around Easter and wait for the gasps of delight. We usually slow roast the shoulder because it maximises the succulence, but for anyone wanting a traditional roast leg, hogget works excellently well for this too.

To serve 4 – 6, you will need:
1 shoulder of hogget, bone in
½ bottle of organic Chardonnay
8 sprigs of rosemary
5 fat cloves of garlic, peeled
extra virgin olive oil

herb topping:
>   1 sprig rosemary
>   2 sprigs thyme
>   2 sprigs winter savory
>   2 sprigs fresh marjoram (or a good pinch dried}
>   black pepper and sea salt

Pre-heat the oven to 180°C. Slice up one of the cloves of garlic and, making some slits in the meat with the point of knife, slip the slivers into the joint at strategic places, making sure you put some close to the bones. Finely chop the herbs for the topping and mix with the freshly ground black pepper and sea salt. In a lidded casserole dish, place the 8 sprigs of rosemary and the other four cloves of garlic. Sprinkle with a good glug of olive oil and. put the shoulder of hogget on top of the herbs. Pour the ½ bottle of Chardonnay around the joint. Sprinkle some more olive oil over the joint and rub it all over, then sprinkle the seasoned chopped herbs evenly over. Put the lid on the casserole and place it in the oven for 20 minutes, after which you can turn the heat down to 140°C and leave it for four hours.

If the meat is not tender and falling off the bones, give it another 30 minutes. Then remove the meat and keep it warm. Strain the fat from the pan juices and discard. Now strain the contents of the pan through a sieve into a small saucepan, bring to the boil and thicken with arrowroot (a bit of a cheat, but it's quick!). Off the heat, stir in a tablespoon of crème fraiche and adjust the seasoning. Serve on a bed of crisp pan-wilted spring cabbage with some golden roasted pink fir apple potatoes which, at Aspen House, would be the last of the winter stocks.

We believe that it is time for a radical rethink of the comfortable habit of 'convenience' shopping. Fifty years of being sold the concept of cheap food conveniently housed under one roof has brought out the worst in society. As the scales tip in favour of the negative aspects of our psyche, our more desirable human characteristics, such as honour, respect, altruism, compassion, generosity, sincerity, truth and even good humour diminish, sometimes sinking so far that they vanish without trace. A return to those positive values is long overdue.

Some say that society is already changing its bad old ways. 'Ethical shopping' has entered the language as one of a clutch of new buzz phrases, but I suggest that in many cases it is no more than that, a trendy phrase, and can even be a dangerous idea in a world still addicted to consumerism. With food shopping, however, it can be clear-cut. Here we have a real chance to do the right thing. We can shop ethically with a clear conscience, because much of what we eat can be bought directly from the person who grows or produces it. Going to a Farmers' Market and buying vegetables direct from the grower cuts out all the links that normally exist in today's buying chain – those links that start with just a single wholesaler, as illustrated in my story of Pershore Growers in the previous chapter.

In running Aspen House, we are committed to the idea of paying a fair price for what we buy. For us, it is the only acceptable ethical stance and unquestionably the right thing to do. We don't live in a perfect world, and it can still be quite difficult to know for certain that we are buying fairly, so these days we always err on the side of caution in order to avoid unwittingly imposing an unfair price on someone. The Fair Trade movement was started in order to raise awareness of the many thousands of farmers, growers and small producers all around the world, especially in Third World countries, upon whom an unfair price is inflicted by global businesses. Laudable as it may be, however, the Fair Trade scheme seems to overlook the fact that this unscrupulous practice happens in our own back yard too, and afflicts thousands of smaller food producers. Western countries are supposedly safe in the arms of Free Trade, as defined by the World Trade Organisation. The reality is that this system benefits big business and exploits small business, whose individual miseries are too small to show up on the economic radar.

Most of this never enters mainstream thinking, so it is difficult for the layman to spot that there is a problem at all, particularly with horticulture or farming, yet it is all too real for our beleaguered farmers. We are losing our agricultural base at a frightening rate, and I believe that this will impinge on our future food security. So let charity begin at home and let us carry our ethical principles right into the Farmers' Market, the farm shop, other independent shops or to the local veg box scheme. Once we embrace the principle of ethical food shopping, then it becomes second nature to demand that our exotic products, such as tea, coffee, chocolate and spices, should also be bought at a price which is fair to the sellers and does not exploit them.

Though we usually frequent the Hereford Farmers' Market, we have been known to forage further afield, even calling in at the Bristol Slow Food Market one Sunday – but then, Bristol market has almost achieved cult status, with stalls that seem to go on for ever, taking over a couple of streets in an old part of the city. It's worth a visit just to find products like saltmarsh lamb and Keen's Cheddar, the latter stacked up two or three truckles deep and scenting the air with the most pleasant aroma which wafts past the stall to mingle with all the other foodie odours.

Altogether more low-key and on a much humbler scale, Monmouth Farmers' Market has an intimate atmosphere, with no more than a dozen small stalls set up on the ancient Monnow Bridge. This is where we go if we want to buy local Trealy Farm charcuterie. Some of their salamis, air-dried hams and chorizo sausage are so good they easily beat the Europeans at their own game.

On one occasion at Monmouth, we saw a new stall selling pork products, proudly displaying the banner, Emma's Pigs. Unfamiliar with the name, we thought we should ask our usual searching questions about provenance, husbandry practices and feeding of the animals. The stall was manned by a woman and two girls, which prompts the question, "Is 'manned' the right word for an all-female crew?" Anyway, leaving semantics aside for the moment, we asked another question.

"So, which one of you is Emma?"

Two sets of fingers pointed towards the youngest of the trio, a quiet girl with a shy smile.

"Emma looks after the pigs," we were told, by way of additional information, "And we do the selling."

"So, what sort of pigs do you keep?" we asked Emma, who answered with another shy smile but no further comment. But she didn't need to, because the hitherto unseen main salesman of the team suddenly appeared under Sally's right elbow. He was a young lad of about twelve years old, brimming with confidence.

"Right," he said in a no-nonsense kind of way, as he moved to our side of the stall to indicate some photos of pigs pinned up under the display cabinet, "We have Berkshires, Saddlebacks, Oxford Sandy and Blacks, and Tamworths. And today the sausages are Saddlebacks."

Well, there was no arguing with that. So we bought a couple of pounds of Saddleback sausages without hesitation with a view to trying them out for breakfast the next morning.

It must be said that we found this brief encounter heart-warmingly human, and we resolved to find out more about Emma and her pigs. From our experience at the market that day, it was clear that this is a family concern, with mother supervising three youngsters who obviously enjoy the job and take it seriously, whilst father is there in the background checking on stock levels and operating the 'till', an old-fashioned lockable cash box. But the story behind this scene is quite unusual.

Firstly, this is not a family of farmers, just a family with a couple of spare acres in west Herefordshire. However, a new journey into animal husbandry began when Emma asked for a couple of Berkshire piglets for her 14th birthday. Her parents obliged, possibly thinking she might grow out of the idea once the rigours of pig-keeping became a reality. But, no, that's not what happened. What happened was that Emma became fascinated by the whole story of how our native breeds have been ousted by the hybridised standard British porker, and she became determined to make a contribution to a slowly reviving interest in our old breeds.

Gradually, numbers grew, and Emma's pigs represented a good cross-section of the best of British breeds: Middle Whites, Tamworths, Oxford Sandy & Blacks, Saddlebacks, Gloucester Old Spots as well as her original Berkshires. Inevitably, the whole family was soon involved in Emma's new enterprise, and committed to providing the pigs with the best possible life. Paradoxically, the one sure way of preserving these breeds is to use them for meat, and it is fortunate that one of the county's few remaining local abattoirs is quite close. The slower, more sympathetic approach of this old-fashioned establishment means that the pigs are guaranteed a stress-free exit from a stress-free life. Modern intensively reared animals have no such luck, living a short, brutish and stressful life that ends in pain and fear.

Emma's little business continues to grow and has now branched out into the manufacture of pig arks, running pig-keeping courses and offering their own unique 'Own a Pig' scheme, whereby anyone who wants their own pig but doesn't have the space for one can have it reared at Emma's place, eventually having it delivered in edible form. Emma, along with her older sister, Claire, and her younger brother, Ben (chief salesman!), as well as her two extremely supportive parents, is now committed to her desire to work with traditional British pig breeds. It is wonderful to see such enthusiasm for what is a difficult job involving a lot of hard work, and it was equally wonderful to see Emma's Pigs proudly flying their banner in Monmouth that day.

With the Farmers' Market set up on the old bridge in clear view of the dominant Waitrose store at that end of town, it is an act of defiance and a statement of intent for the market's customers to go to the trouble to walk just that little bit further to buy some sausages and bacon from Emma and her family. The money that changed hands on Emma's stall that day will 'stay local' whereas, despite Waitrose's protestations that it is part of the John Lewis Partnership and therefore not beholden to shareholders, most of the money spent at their Monmouth branch leaves the community.

Besides, buying sausages from Emma's stall means bringing just another little bit of human contact back into our lives. Waitrose insists that human contact is part of what makes them different, and that their staff are like one big happy family. But, just because it is possible to see the same people pushing a snake of trolleys around the car park each week, this is not a family, and shopping at Waitrose is not the same as dealing with Emma. The familiar trolley pusher is a waged employee (albeit a 'partner') working for a big out-of-town business;

Emma and her family are running a newly-fledged local business and are now facing the challenge of surviving in a world that mostly can't be bothered with the likes of them. Supermarket buyers don't want them because they are too small to deal with, and the buying public don't want them because they are seduced by the bright lights of the Waitrose emporium. But I can tell you that the human contact with such hard-working people, whose goal is to deliver the finest meat for our tables, is more valuable than anything the supermarket can ever hope to sell. Shopping like it used to be, maybe, and shopping with all the 'inconvenience' of dealing with different people for different purchases, but shopping with a soul – priceless.

It's the first Saturday in the month and time for the Hereford Farmers' Market once again. We head into town to see our favourite stallholders. Before ethics dictated that we could no longer find it acceptable to shop at a supermarket, we would have been driving to the big Tesco on the outskirts of town to load up our trolley. It is now many years since we did that, but we do not miss it at all. I sometimes liken it to being released from the shackles that bound me to a wild-eyed lunatic. We do not miss the much-trumpeted 'convenience,' actually finding it just as convenient to shop at the Farmers' Market and the independent shops nearby. And, yes, we would have been the first to be sceptical about the idea that shopping at independents could ever be convenient, but we are happy to have been proved wrong. It is always satisfying to see an urban myth exposed for what it is.

Because we are buying only what we need, most of which is pre-ordered anyway, we find that we spend so little time in town that we can always fit in a break for a coffee and a scone. Our regular haunts are all independently owned, such as Bill's café in All Saints church, the Green Café in St Owen Street and, just lately, Gomati's in Aubrey Street. Money spent in any of these establishments stays in the community, unlike money spent in the High Street chains like Costa or Starbucks. Despite their much-trumpeted and possibly quite laudable support for Fair Trade, both these well-known names are global corporations in their own right, with Costa being part of the giant

Whitbread conglomerate. Though outwardly portraying a cosy friendly image, their facades hide standard corporate practices. Even if they were squeaky clean, they still suck money out of the local communities in which they have a presence, so we will not support them. And the alternatives are there. Any town or city that is big enough to have a Costa or a Starbucks is big enough to have at least one independent café or tea room, where it should be possible to get a decent cup of something and a home made cake. Look around your own town – you might be pleasantly surprised. And if they don't offer home made cakes, ask them why not.

The stallholders we visit are now like old friends, as are the people who work in the local wholefood shops. Rather than being a chore or a drudge, shopping in this way is like being on holiday in Europe. Everything is relaxed, and life takes on a gentler pace. Paradoxically, it feels as if we have all the time in the world drifting through the market at this pace, yet in reality we move quickly from stall to stall. We can't dawdle too much, because every stall is busy and we would be interrupting the flow of trade. Though our conversations at each stall are short, the fact that we have them at all is so much more uplifting than trying to conduct a transaction with a mind-numbed checkout operator. True human contact is becoming ever more elusive in this fast-paced automated modern world of ours, and it is good for the soul to be able to speak to real people.

We return home with enough bacon and sausage from the Tudge family to carry us through to the next market in two weeks time, as well as some black pudding and gorgeous orange-yolked bantam eggs from Sue Fletcher on the game stall, plus maybe some fresh vegetables from Enid from Tillington Court Farm and a new plant for the garden from Dave Griffiths, the local nurseryman. All the money we have spent stays in local hands and will more than likely be spent in the local community again. Unlike the money spent in a supermarket, it won't leave the local area and return to head office to be distributed to shareholders and executives with six-figure salaries. As we round off the day back at home by getting the kettle on and having our last cuppa of the day, we feel refreshed by our excursion to the market, satisfied that we have stocked up on some fabulous produce and morally uplifted by the knowledge that we are helping to support these people who have become our friends, people who represent the kind of producers that we will all need more and more as our world heads towards an unknown future and an almost certain food crisis.

Jadwiga's chocolate soufflé cake with strawberries and cream (Sally's version)

I could take any recipe and discuss the ethical implications of choosing the ingredients but I decided on this one because not only has it been given to me by Rob's Mum, to whom this book is dedicated, but it is simple to make and it involves chocolate and strawberries - everybody's favourite! So for a truly ethical dessert, this is how to source the ingredients.

Two ingredients we can't source locally need to be sporting the Fairtrade logo, and they are chocolate and sugar. The growing and production of both these products is open to abuse, so to be sure that land and people are not being exploited in their production, this logo is the nearest we can get to helping us to make an ethical purchase. Where they also carry an organic label, so much the better.

If you can find Divine chocolate (widely sold now, but particularly in Oxfam shops) you can be assured that your money will be helping the Ghanaian co-operative Kuapa Kokoo to invest in a better future. The full story is printed on the inside of the chocolate bar wrapper. The other bonus of course is that these farmers grow cocoa as it should be grown, in the shade of the tropical rainforest, thus ensuring a truly efficacious product.

The eggs should come from hens that have been allowed to behave naturally and which have been given the freedom to roam and forage. The cream and butter should come from cows that are feeding on organic pasture in spring and summer and on hay and silage in the winter. Finally strawberries should preferably be sourced from a small organic producer who grows his fruit outdoors, not in polytunnels. Strawberries are a summer fruit, and therefore have all the vitality of the sun locked up in their flesh, ready to be released when we take that first bite.

For this cake you will need:
100g plain chocolate (nothing under 70%)
100g unsalted butter
4 large eggs separated
75g caster sugar
250ml double cream
250g strawberries

Butter the bottom and sides of an 8" springform tin and line the bottom and sides with baking parchment. Break up the chocolate and place with the butter in a pudding basin over a saucepan of barely simmering water. Stir gently until the chocolate has melted and then remove from the heat. Meanwhile whisk the egg yolks and, when the chocolate is cool, gradually incorporate the yolks into the chocolate and butter until blended. Follow this with the sugar, taking care not to overwork the chocolate. In a bowl, beat the egg whites until stiff peaks form when the beater is withdrawn. Fold this into the chocolate mixture and then pour into the prepared tin.

Bake in a preheated oven at 160°C for about an hour or until a cake tester inserted into the centre comes out clean. Place on a wire rack to cool for 5 minutes then with a small spatula loosen the edges and turn out onto a rack. Cool completely. The cake will sink slightly in the centre but don't worry as this provides you with a great opportunity to fill it with something delicious! When you are ready to serve (and this cake can be made the day before), whip up the cream until stiff and fill the indented surface leaving the edges free. Hull and quarter the strawberries and arrange them over the top of the cream. You could always finish off the effect by garnishing with chocolate curls.

Chapter Five

Eat . . . sensually

There is a scene in Mike Leigh's film, *Life is Sweet*, where Jane Horrocks, playing an anorexic girl called Nicola, asks her emotionally stunted boyfriend, played by David Thewlis, to lick chocolate off her pale naked body. Sadly for some, no doubt, this is not what I mean when I talk about eating sensually. Neither am I talking about feeding your blindfolded partner strawberries or chillies, or indeed getting up to any of the tricks that Mickey Rourke tried with Kim Basinger in the over-hyped and ultimately dreary *9½ Weeks*. I would concede, however, that some of the scenes in *Babette's Feast, Fried Green Tomatoes* or *Chocolat* have a certain sensuality about them, in a truly human interpretation of the word 'sensual.' And that's what I am talking about – allowing your senses to work together to elevate the spirit and to make the whole experience of eating a delight.

Without the senses engaged, food can so easily become merely fuel and nothing more. Food is nourishment, but as much for the soul as for the body. For the fortunate, it is a daily event, so it seems churlish not to make the most of it and to employ our senses in creating a fuller experience and understanding of the spiritual nature of what we eat. Ideally, eating should be part of a process which embraces preparation and cooking, for then we can bring all five senses, including hearing, into play. Was there ever a sound more agreeable than the sizzle of a roast as it is taken from the oven, or even the sound of onions frying in a pan? We can see, touch, smell and taste our food as we prepare it for the table, but there is something fundamentally satisfying about also hearing the sounds of preparation, stirring up ancient subliminal memories of fire pits and the warmth and security they symbolise.

Placki ('platski') – Polish potato pancakes

As a sensual culinary experience, it is hard to beat these fantastic little treats – something akin to a cross between a potato cake and a plain rösti. As with all such traditions, there are many variations on the theme, so I am going to give you my own, developed from the version my mother taught me.

Be warned . . . if you do these for the family, they will disappear as fast as you can make them, and chips will never taste the same again! So let's just start with a small quantity – enough to make, say, twelve. For that you will need six medium sized potatoes (floury are best, but waxy will work too), a dessertspoon of unbleached flour, one egg and some good sea salt and freshly ground black pepper.

Peel and grate the potatoes into a bowl, using the medium side of the grater. Don't do this in the food processor, because it doesn't have the right effect. In any case, this is a sensual experience, and you need to engage with your food!

Once grated, tip the potato into a sieve and rinse under the tap to get rid of most of the starch. Then squeeze the remaining liquid from the grated potato, a handful at a time, putting the potato back in the bowl. Add the egg and flour and season well with salt and pepper before mixing thoroughly with a wooden spoon, or your fingers if you prefer.

Heat some oil to just below smoking point and test with a small bit of the mixture. If you get a satisfying sizzle, the oil is ready for frying. Using a dessertspoon, take a small ball from the mixture, put it in the oil and flatten it out with the back of the spoon to form a thin pancake. Put in as many as your pan will comfortably hold without the platski touching and fry until the edges begin to go brown, then turn and brown the other side.

If you are brave enough to try to keep up with demand, serve them straight from the pan to the clamouring hordes queuing up in the kitchen. Otherwise, to preserve decorum, put them to drain on kitchen paper on a plate in a warm oven and serve them three to a plate with a little tossed salad on the side and a dollop of crème fraiche on top.

For an even more authentic taste, and when cucumbers and garden dill are truly seasonal in the summer, serve the platski with *miseria*, another stunning Polish idea.

Miseria

Peel a cucumber, then slice it paper thin into a bowl. Sprinkle it with sea salt and leave it for an hour or so, until the slices of cucumber are completely wilted. Taking a small handful of cucumber at a time, squeeze out the moisture and put the cucumber into a clean bowl. Add some chopped fresh dill and a few dessertspoons of crème fraiche or sour cream. Stir to mix thoroughly and serve alongside the platski. If there is anything that will make people want to eat more platski, it is the presence of a bowl of miseria to go with them!

You have been warned.

In my lifelong involvement with the culinary arts, I have developed a bit of a thing about eggs and, yes, they appeal to me on a sensual level. Maybe it's because the first eggs I can remember tasting were from the hens wandering around in Grandpa's farmyard, or maybe it's because, once Grandpa had retired, we had our own chickens at the bottom of the garden when I was a teenager. Whatever the reason, eggs to me are wondrous. One of Nature's perfect foods, eggs are delivered in their own biodegradable packaging, thus making them eminently transportable from henhouse to kitchen.

Whether they come from traditional farmyard hens, diminutive bantams, Guinea fowl, ducks or geese, the sight of them is a delight. On one occasion, filled with the zeal more normally associated with Victorian butterfly collectors, Sally and I went to the trouble of visiting as many local suppliers as possible within a 10-mile radius of Aspen House, and we came back with a fine selection from Cotswold Legbars, Cream Legbars, Araucanas, Black Rocks, Leghorns, Wyandottes and Marans. The colours ranged from the white of the Leghorns to the very dark brown, almost brick red, of the Marans. Between these two extremes was a pastel palette to rival a Farrow & Ball colour chart, ranging from pale blue to cream to pinkish speckled to pale terracotta. They all looked spectacular in a basket together.

Using these eggs at breakfast adds another dimension to the pleasure of cooking, and it makes no difference if I am cooking for a house full of guests or just the two of us. To me, the eggs I use are gifts from Nature and I respect both them and the hens that gave them up. Call me sentimental, but I believe fundamentally that we are as much a part of the natural process of Planet Earth as any of the animals on it. I cannot read John Donne's famous lines that suggest all human beings are part of the same family without seeing that actually it goes much further than this; I see that all Nature is one.

John Donne : Meditation 17 – Devotions upon Emergent Occasions

"No man is an Island, entire of it self; every man is a piece of the Continent, a part of the main; if a clod be washed away by the sea, Europe is the less, as well as if a promontory were, as well as if a manor of thy friends or of thine own were; any man's death diminishes me, because I am involved in Mankind; and therefore never send to know for whom the bell tolls; it tolls for thee."

Whenever we have guests to breakfast, I stand at our six-burner gas hob and cook the finest local eggs. Most guests order a cooked breakfast which includes them. Even after all these years, their preparation and cooking are imbued with what you might call a quiet reverence, and the sensuality of it is not lost on me. Even the look of the shell touches me – I marvel at the process of actually creating such an object. With some of the attractive pastel eggs, I feel it is almost a sacrilege to crack the shell, but at least I know it will be returned to Nature via the compost heap.

I have a method of frying eggs that seems to bring out all that is good about them, and I cannot deny the way my senses respond to what it involves, from the gentle fizz of fresh butter in the pan to the sight of the transparent albumen beginning to solidify into white as the egg settles into the melted butter. Then there is the sizzle as I add a splash of water to the pan and cover it with a lid. This gently steams the top of the egg, allowing it to cook through without going hard on the bottom. As I lift the lid, the aroma, a combination of egg and butter, makes me wish it is my breakfast I am cooking . . . and on Sundays, it is. Eggs, along with bacon, sausage and black pudding create a plateful that is such a delight we make sure we indulge ourselves once a week, and the pleasure of this weekly treat is really beyond words.

> *"Never work before breakfast; if you have to work before breakfast, eat your breakfast first."*
>
> Josh Billings

Our senses are of course driven by instinct, which has developed from our need to survive. Though instinct works at an innate level, it relies on our outward senses for confirmation of instinctual decisions. Let me give you an example, whilst I am talking about eggs.

I was once given half a dozen from a supplier with whom I was not acquainted, but I was assured that they were really good, organic and from a small flock. When it came to using them for cooking, however, my observation was that they were not as good as those I get from our own two regular suppliers. Don't get me wrong. They were lovely and fresh – and obviously not from the supermarket. But as soon as I cracked one into the pan, I could see that it was not quite right. The yolk, although deep yellow in colour, looked dull. Although barely perceptible, the yolk was shrouded in a vaguely opaque film. By contrast, my usual eggs have yolks that are very bright, deep in colour, and covered by a glossy film that is quite transparent.

My conclusion was that the birds that laid them were being fed a controlled diet, albeit organic. I suspected that their feed was also enriched with carotenoids to give the yolks that colour. Most egg marketing authorities these days require egg yolks to be somewhere between deep yellow and orange. To put it into industry terminology, egg yolk colour 'is expected to be in the range of 9 to 12 on the DSM Yolk Colour Fan.' For me, this paints a picture that I find deeply disturbing, but that's business for you. The egg marketing authorities recognise that customers judge the quality of an egg by the colour of its yolk, hence it is common practice to ensure that feed has sufficient carotenoids in it. If yolk colour is too pale, the remedy is simple. To quote from one of the leading poultry websites, www.thepoultrysite.com "Yolk colour in laying hens is primarily determined by the content and profile of pigmenting carotenoids present in their feed and can easily be adapted via feed ingredients to match consumer preferences."

This sets me jangling with indignation again at the interference by outside agencies of dubious authority trying to improve on nature with their ideas, and to disguise something inferior in order to deceive us. But it doesn't work. What should be done is to allow hens to be able to behave naturally and forage for their food. As soon as interference takes place, something goes wrong and our senses can spot it a mile off. We can see that the colour of the yolk is artificial in some way and we can taste the difference.

It could be argued that it is easy for me, because I am cooking with eggs virtually every day, but I maintain that using our senses like this is natural, and comes naturally to us, as it does to all other creatures. For instance, when the raspberries in the garden are in season, the birds, just like us, want the berries that are just reaching perfection. They have no interest in the old, misshapen or shrivelled ones. It is obvious to them, as it is to us, that these have no appeal. And all fruit and vegetables deteriorate once they pass their peak of perfection. Even carrots and potatoes progressively lose their sheen once they have been lifted from the ground, as most of us are aware.

So, despite all the efforts of the food industry, we still have some inherent ability to be able to judge the worth of a food. It is no doubt a basic trait that we have developed through evolution which will have helped to keep our species successful. We should trust that instinct, and the senses that inform it. Sight, touch, smell and taste should tell us if something is good to eat, and in addition we have generations of accumulated knowledge to call on. Industry treats food as a commodity, but it is too valuable for that. Of all our precious resources, food is the one that actually keeps us alive. Gradually, we are waking up to all that is precious about food, but progress is slow. Though we are already nearing the end of the first decade of the 21st Century, we are still encumbered with the bad habits of the previous century. Before we lose our farming, our food heritage and our food-related skills altogether, it is imperative that we learn to sharpen up our senses, revive our instinct and learn to understand our true relationship with food, a relationship we have been developing since the day we first walked the Earth.

From those earliest days, we have had to obtain enough food from our immediate surroundings to sustain us from generation to generation. Beginning as hunter-gatherers, we learned about wild foods in the form of nuts, berries and a wide variety of plant-based foods. Later we learned how to stalk, trap and kill animals, eating their meat as a high-protein and high fat supplement to what must have generally been a meagre diet. As our skills developed, we learned that if we constructed fences to keep animals confined, it would be easier to kill one when needed without having to scour the grasslands for the next big meal. With the semi-permanence of these animal pens, our nomadic existence slowed down. We soon applied the same principles to plants. Cultivation of plants and grains became the new preoccupation, and a rudimentary form of agriculture was born.

Some would argue, very convincingly, that this is where the rot set in as far as the human race is concerned. It has been called humanity's worst invention, and it has been said that, by radically changing the way we acquire our food, it has condemned us to live a life that becomes increasingly inferior. Proponents of this argument go as far as to say that agriculture has led directly to large-scale war, inequality, poverty, crime, famine and human-induced climate change. That's quite an argument, and not one to which I would raise any serious objections, but it is beyond the scope of this book to examine it in any detail.

One aspect of that argument which is irrefutable, however, is that, in terms of human values, we have lost more than we have gained since moving on from our hunter-gatherer existence. Some might see this as a fatuous comment when it is so obvious to them that we now live in a land of plenty, but such abundance has come at a very high price, mainly in terms of the human and social values that we once held so dear. Modern life has made us more insular, introspective and isolated. Unlike us, those hunter-gatherers who can still be found in the more remote parts of our world have lost none of their human values. They work together and their communities are mutually supportive, as co-operation and sharing are vital in both hunting and gathering. They live in small, egalitarian, consensus-based, happy communities. Far from living the life of the savage as popularly depicted by literature and the propaganda of Hollywood, these people have rightly been described as 'the original affluent society' (Marshall Sahlins, 1966), rich in all those things that make human life worth living. We in the modern world, by contrast, have lost the plot. We spend our discontented lives chasing our tails, selling our precious and limited time on this Earth to the highest bidder, in order to acquire all those things which we have been told will make us happy: a bigger house, a bigger car or another foreign holiday in some over-developed coastal resort. It is an indictment of our industrialised society that the second biggest currency in the world today is Airmiles.

The original affluent society

To quote from Marshall Sahlins:
"Hunter-gatherers consume less energy per capita per year than any other group of human beings. Yet, when you come to examine it, the original affluent society was none other than the hunter's – in which all the people's material wants were easily satisfied. To accept that hunters are affluent is therefore to recognise that the present human condition of man slaving to bridge the gap between his unlimited wants and his insufficient means is a tragedy of modern times."

At its basic level, contentment comes from having enough food, warmth and shelter, but we lost our grip on this essential principle many centuries ago, and it would seem the situation since then has become progressively worse. Many people today would agree that life has become uncomfortably stressful in the industrialised world. For some, emotions are stretched to breaking point as they juggle careers, children, activities, social commitments and money worries. In the worst-case scenario, many feel trapped in a day-to-day existence over which they have no control, and phrases like 'rat race', 'hamster cage' and 'on the treadmill' are used to describe it. The typical traditional hunter-gatherer, on the other hand, works for about three hours a day, quite possibly in the company of his best friends from the same community. The rest of his time is his own, and he uses it to eat, relax, visit friends, play with his children, or to sit around making music, telling stories, philosophising or just sleeping.

Unhappily, for those of us who live in an industrialised society, this kind of easy life has nearly gone forever. All we have now is the adman's version of it, sold to us relentlessly in the shape of holidays and 'leisure activities'. Disappointingly, the adman's version is a mirage, with no more substance than morning mist, burned off by the harsh glare of the daily grind. On a more positive note, though, there is something we can do about it, and that is what I am talking about in these pages. We can slow down, review our relationship with food and open the box in which our senses have been hiding. It's not perfect, but it's a good start. Though we cannot yet recreate the relaxed world of the hunter-gatherer, we can make our own daily lives more pleasurable in the meantime by bringing food back to the top of the agenda. Taking the steps that are being discussed in this book changes our perception of what food actually is. It revives our dormant senses and gives instinct a proper role again.

Instinct, and the five senses that support it, are fantastically valuable resources, demeaned and diminished by those who would rather we didn't use them at all. After all, if we used our senses every time we see those TV ads for factory foods, wouldn't we just shun such fare without further question? Of course we would. So the marketing professionals have had to devise messages that are more powerful than those delivered by our own good sense. Faced with a cup of instant coffee, common sense should tell you that it is going to taste awful, that the only thing about it that resembles real coffee is the aroma that leaves the jar when you pull off the foil top and that the drink you make from it is never going to be as good as a cup of real coffee. Nevertheless, the marketing that sells it to us is full of emotive imagery, well-chosen words, lots of smiling faces and the implication in pictures that this particular brand of instant coffee is going to create for you an exotic world beyond your wildest dreams. This kind of hypnotism is very hard to ignore.

Let your instinct in and use your senses. They will *tell* you that instant coffee is not very exciting. And they will tell you the same about all those other brand-name factory foods. Trust your senses – they know best. Buttery Flora? It's no better for you than any other kind of Flora. If you want something that tastes like butter, *use real butter.* We must not let our food choices be made for us by a businessman who wants to sell us something. We should be making our own food choices. It's time to rethink our shopping and avoid inferior imitation foods.

We should trust our senses and our instinct, and reserve our mistrust for those who would sell us inferior food. We should not allow them, or the 'science' that backs them, to have the only opinion about what is good and what is not and what degree of goodness is acceptable. Science has become a little too cocky of late and it needs to remember who its parents are – instinct and experience. We must give these the respect they deserve, considering they are what kept us alive before science came along. When buying a ready meal with an appetising picture on the package, we know instinctively that the food inside, in its little plastic compartments and sachets, is going to taste like the junk it really is. Yet we shut our eyes tight and cover our other senses and just tell ourselves that the gloopy mess on our plates is as good as the picture on the box. It is time to open our eyes again, bring our senses into play and move one step closer towards repairing our relationship with food.

We are sensual beings and sensual pleasure is what drives us. But I am not talking about the fleeting flashes of our glitzy techno world. This is good fun, but it is not fundamental. For true sensual pleasure that really touches the soul, preparing, cooking and sharing food with others is a great start. Choosing foods that are the most appropriate for the season and having the confidence to cook without a recipe opens the door to the Zen elements of food. Without a doubt, there is a need to master basic culinary skills, but this is not as difficult as it might seem and, once mastered, we can soar, creating food that stirs our senses, gives us pleasure and nourishes our souls.

Cooking without a recipe . . .

This might look like a recipe, but it isn't. It's just a way of making a basic homely broth. We often do this in the winter months when we want something nourishing and easy to make. The idea is to use whatever fresh vegetables you can find, put them together in a soup and to understand what needs to be done to the soup to make it tasty.

So, firstly there is no need to worry about stock. If your vegetables are fresh and organic, they will have plenty of taste. You can use whatever seasonal vegetables you can find locally, but carrots, parsnips, celeriac and potatoes all work well together.

Put a handful of red lentils in a big pot, cover them with water and bring to the boil. While this is happening, peel and dice up a couple of carrots, a parsnip, a thick slice of celeriac and, if you like, a medium sized potato. Once the lentils have come to the boil, put in all the vegetables, add some more water and simmer until they soften – around 15 minutes. The idea is not to overcook them, hence the need to dice them up. The more they cook, the more nutrition they lose.

As the soup is simmering, chop an onion and fry it in olive oil until it softens and takes on a golden colour. The onion is your taste catalyst. It will lift all the other flavours and bring them to life. When the onion is soft and golden, add it to the soup with any residue of olive oil – it's all tasty stuff. Now add a few crushed garlic cloves (we use about six) and season with sea salt and freshly ground black pepper.

Good locally produced organic garlic will not only add taste but also is excellent for your immune system in the winter. For this reason, we don't cook the soup after we have added the garlic. Don't worry about the taste of raw garlic; you will find that the heat of the soup will simply eliminate the raw flavour.

Served with some home made bread, this is quite moreish, and you can vary the theme next time you do the soup. For instance, try adding some cumin seeds to the onions while they are cooking and then adding the juice of half a lemon to the soup. Or adding a tin of chopped tomatoes to the onions once they are cooked. Simmer onions and tomatoes together for five minutes before adding to the soup.

If you want to add some greenery, sprinkle with chopped parsley (if you can find any in the winter!) or just add some sliced leeks that have been gently softened in butter for five minutes. Let the leeks cool before adding to the hot soup. That way they will preserve their green colour while you eat.

The message is: just experiment with different ideas, different flavours and see what happens – its all part of the fun.

Chapter Six

Eat . . . joyfully

The first Christmas I can clearly remember remains to this day a memory full of wonder and joy. Of all the Christmases that have come and gone since then, many have been equally memorable occasions but, for me, there is nothing to replace the memory of that first experience of something truly special.

I can't really recall how old I was, or even where I was, but that does not matter. What fills my head with vivid pictures is the magic, and what made it magical was the combination of food, family, festivity and wonderment. My mother is Polish, and the first Christmas I remember was her version of this most important of occasions. For her, of course, there was the overriding religious element, the celebration of the birth of Christ. At that age, I didn't really understand much about the mystery of faith that enchanted my mother. For me, the enchantment was the atmosphere of anticipation in the house.

It all happened on Christmas Eve, which in itself gives the occasion an extra emotional charge. Think of New Year's Eve or Halloween, once known as All Hallows Eve. The word 'eve' somehow bristles with a sense of anticipation that just doesn't come across with an expression like, 'the day before my birthday'. If we added to our vocabulary phrases such as 'birthday eve' or 'holiday eve', the thrill of expectation might give to those times an indefinable frisson. But perhaps it is only right that we do not do so, for familiarity, as we all know, breeds contempt, like playing your favourite CD over and over again. Ubiquity topples the celebrated from its pinnacle of unattainability and precipitates the commonplace; thus the special is reduced to the banal, like salmon in a supermarket. Perhaps it is as well that the word 'eve' is attached to so few dates in the calendar.

Even now, for me Christmas Eve has a special ring to it, but when I was a child it was truly magical. All day there would be the bustle of domestic activity in the kitchen, the culmination of several days' work, as my mother, my *babcia* (my Polish granny) and any other willing helpers would prepare dish after dish for the supper table. Practically from the time I could walk, I was one of those helpers, encouraged by the elders to get involved in the whole process. As an aside, it has to be said that it is to society's detriment that we have lost our way in passing on ancient culinary skills. At one time, it was just the way things were done, each generation teaching the next one by example. Thus, by the time I came to cook my own Christmas Eve supper, I knew what to do, because I had been shown the way. Nowadays, so little gets shown, because there is so little knowledge to pass on. However, I digress.

Though supper was the central theme, this was more than a meal. It was simply a joyous uplifting of the soul in celebration of the family and new life. To what might be called the untrained eye, a Polish Christmas Eve supper has the appearance of a veritable feast, a serious banquet. Intriguingly, it is looked upon by the Poles themselves as the culmination of a day of fasting. The meal contains no meat, thus maintaining that symbol of abstinence until communion at Midnight Mass. Yet the meal would last for hours. Twelve courses, one for each of the apostles, would be brought to table that night, with the festivities beginning as soon as the first star shone in the sky. As the day waned into twilight, my brother and I would station ourselves at the window, our hearts quickening with excitement as we stared at the reddening Western sky waiting for that first twinkle.

Unable to contain our impatience, we would sometimes point and cry out, each of us wanting to be the first to claim the prize of seeing bright Venus wink through the darkness. My mother would respond to our gesticulations by coming to the window and checking for herself. Our disappointment was hard to bear if she told us in soft Polish tones that we were imagining things. But there was no mistaking that glorious evening star once it became clearly visible. Time to sit and eat!

With everything set out on a crisp white tablecloth, the sense of formality was inescapable, yet the tingle of joy in the air was palpable. With all the family sitting together around the table, faces lit by the glow of candlelight, and the Christmas tree hung with home made decorations, it was clear to me even as a young child that this was a very special time. It was a time of friendship and humanity, a time for banishing quarrels, a time for forgiveness, all of which was impressed upon us by the family elders. The hand of succour was extended to any lonely traveller who might be passing, with a flickering candle in the window as a guiding light and a place reserved at table in case someone should knock at the door. Many years later, when I was grown up and had children of my own, I would impress these customs on them as they were explained to me. In maintaining the tradition of the Christmas Eve supper, we too would set a place for the uninvited guest. What a delight it was one year when someone actually called unexpectedly and we were able to offer him a 12-course supper! For true joy, however, nothing beats the fact that my eldest son, George, once he had set himself up in a home of his own, took to producing Polish Christmas Eve suppers himself, thus keeping the tradition alive.

Of the twelve courses, the one that impressed me the most as a child was the first course, *barszcz*, a glistening deep ruby clear beetroot soup. I suppose you might call this one of the defining moments in my culinary education. During the time that preparations were made in the kitchen, I was fascinated as a child by the transformations that were taking place. I would watch beetroots being sliced into strips and put into a big pot with other vegetables, such as onions, carrots, celery and cabbage, and later I would see the colourful but otherwise uninspiring liquid being strained off. By the time it had been seasoned and brought to table, however, alchemy had taken place and that unexceptional liquid had become a sublime start to the best supper of the year.

Polish Christmas Eve beetroot soup (barszcz)

Ingredients
4 medium sized beetroots
1 carrot, scrubbed clean and cut into chunks
2 slices of celeriac, peeled and cut into strips
1 large onion, peeled and sliced
2-3 cabbage leaves, roughly sliced
4 large pieces of dried mushroom
2 bay leaves
2 thick stalks of parsley
sea salt
cider or perry vinegar

SERVES 6 – 8

Wash and peel the beets, then cut into julienne strips. Put the beets into a saucepan with the other vegetables, the mushroom, the bay leaves and parsley stalks. Cover with water, bring to the boil and simmer gently for about 40 minutes.

Strain the soup, retaining the liquid and discarding the vegetables. Traditionally, the foundation of barszcz is *kwas*, the sour liquid obtained by fermenting beets, but I do a shortcut for this Christmas Eve version by seasoning the soup with vinegar. Do it to your own taste, but the idea is to just give the soup a bit of a sharp edge without impinging on the sweetness of the beets. Finally, just adjust the flavour with a sprinkle of sea salt. For a real Christmas Eve feel, serve with *uszki* (little ears), tiny mushroom filled ravioli.

Uszki

Ingredients
4oz unbleached flour
salt and freshly ground black pepper
1 egg
1 tbs water
Filling
2 dried mushrooms
4 fresh brown button mushrooms
1 large shallot
1 tsp chopped dried dill
1 tbs dried breadcrumbs
sea salt and freshly ground black pepper

a good knob of butter

MAKES ABOUT 45

To make the dough, sift flour into a large bowl and season with salt
and pepper. Make a well in the centre and add the egg and water.
Knead the dough by hand until smooth, then wrap it in cling film and
refrigerate it while you make the filling.

For the filling, soak the dried mushrooms in hot water until they are
fully re-hydrated, then chop very finely, reserving the liquid. Chop the
fresh mushrooms and the shallot very finely and sauté gently in the
butter until the shallot begins to colour. Add the dried mushrooms
and their liquid, turn up the heat and stir fry to reduce the liquid by
half. Stir in the dill and the breadcrumbs. Season to taste. Take it off
the heat.

Now divide the dough into 8 pieces. Roll out each piece very thinly.
Cut the sheet of dough into 2" squares. Taking one square at a time,
place a teaspoonful of the filling in the centre of the square and fold
the square into a triangle, crimping the edges together. Then fold the
two corners of the longest (diagonal) edge, so that they overlap,
crimping them together. Set them aside on a floured board while you
make the rest.

Once all the uszki are made, bring a large pan of salted water to the boil and drop the uszki in, stirring them gently to prevent them from sticking to each other. Bring the water back to the boil and simmer the uszki for about three minutes. When they float to the surface they are cooked. Remove them with a slotted spoon, drain and pop three into each bowl of barszcz before taking to the table.

Other courses followed, which might have included stuffed cabbage leaves and mushroom sauce, *pierogi* (Polish ravioli) stuffed with potatoes and cheese or sauerkraut and mushrooms, fish dishes plus cakes and desserts at the end. But all I really remember from that first Christmas is the *barszcz* and the magic. My memories of other Christmas Eve suppers, including the many I hosted for my own family, are cumulative and have been built onto this early foundation. What has never left me is the joy.

I have tried to carry that joy throughout my life. Each meal I eat, however humble, is special to me. My ability to see it like this has been enhanced through the experience of going hungry at certain times in the past. On one occasion, for instance, hitch-hiking through France in the summer holidays with my school friend, John, we ran out of money and therefore also ran out of food. In the last three days of our holiday, we shared a long baguette and some Port Salut cheese – and that was about it. On arrival in Dover, we were fantasising about food in a big way, to the extent that we though of little else as we talked ecstatically about the meal my mum was going to have ready for us as soon as we managed to get back home. Meanwhile, the intensity of our hunger was matched only by the depth of the well of impecuniosity into which we had fallen. Heading out of town, I spotted a bar of Cadbury's Dairy Milk that someone had dropped in the gutter. It had been there some time, and the purple wrapper had faded to pink. The confectionary inside was wearing an ominous white coat which would have looked good on a round of Brie but didn't suit chocolate at all. Undeterred, I broke the bar in two and we both ate it like starving wolves. Despite the fact that this was no more than cheap confectionery well past its best, we consumed it with relish. I have no wish to be that hungry again, and this experience alone taught me to value food. I understood at that moment that if we are hungry enough we will eat anything. Now I have such respect for food that I cannot leave anything I have put on my plate. I eat it joyfully and gratefully. Or, to put it another way, the lesson I learned is that we don't appreciate the worth of those fundamental aspects of life that we so easily take for granted until they are taken from us. As Joni Mitchell says in *Big Yellow Taxi*, "You don't know what you've got 'til it's gone."

Many other isolated incidents from my childhood tell me that our national attitude to food has changed for the worse. When did food stop being pleasurable and become something that is almost an irritation, something that gets in the way of our busy lives, something that takes precious time from activities in which we indulge in the belief that they will make us happy? When did we lose the joy?

I dismiss any criticism that I have fallen into the trap of nostalgia. I don't need to be wearing rose-tinted glasses to know that the joy of food has virtually gone, and taken with it something important, something essentially human. To take just one example, as a young boy I remember a long journey on a train. The journey being over two days, we were on a sleeper train and we had a meal in the dining car. I can remember the white linen tablecloths, the silver cutlery and the waiter dressed formally in white monkey jacket and dark trousers, treating his role with the gravitas it deserved. Mostly I remember the food. Though I cannot tell you now what I ate that day, I can recall the pleasure of the occasion and the feeling that the food had been prepared by someone with a keen knowledge of the culinary arts. By contrast, we probably all have a memory of what followed once the railways were 'modernised'. That icon of 'progress', the dry and lifeless British Rail sandwich, curling at the edges and providing material for countless comedy references over the last few decades, epitomises the decline in our relationship with food. When I think of the roving buffet trolley that defines present-day train travel, wheeled through overcrowded carriages by disconsolate underpaid employees, and offering passengers (sorry – 'customers') nothing but an uninspiring selection of industrialised snacks, I know for sure that there is now no joy in eating on the train. That is, of course, unless you are prepared to pay the inflated prices of first-class travel, in which case, on selected services, you might still find some vestige of what a dining car might have looked like.

> *"One cannot think well, love well, sleep well,*
> *if one has not dined well."*
>
> Virginia Woolf [1882 – 1941]

Even an event as ordinary as going to my Aunty Lil's for tea was a joyous occasion, in honour of which my aforementioned aunt would polish up the best crockery, bake a cake and prepare some sandwiches with the crusts cut off. Aunty Lil lived in Roath Park in Cardiff and worked as a telephone operator at the local exchange, although she did have another life as a chorus singer with the Welsh National Opera. On a daily basis, though, an ordinary job and an ordinary life in a small terraced house in Cardiff. Yet Aunty Lil pushed the boat out when it came to afternoon tea for visiting family. Knowing what I know now about the industrialisation of our food, I would have to suggest that the cake she baked was no doubt made with poor quality bleached flour, but Aunty Lil didn't know that, any more than she knew that the white bread she used for her dainty sandwiches was made from equally degraded flour. But there was no denying the ceremony of the occasion, or the joy with which we all tucked into our tea and cake. Sometimes there might be home made scones or Welsh cakes, always served with a little home made jam. Unwittingly, Aunty Lil was providing a meal that contained minimal nutrition, but the food also served another purpose. It was there as a catalyst for pleasure – the pleasure emanating from a small family gathering of relations who met less frequently than they would have liked. Drinking tea from the best china and eating freshly made sandwiches and cakes gave the gathering a sense of occasion, creating small but significant memories. The fact that I am writing about it all these years later tells me something about how pleasurably food and human bonding work together. In this fast-paced modern world, we would do well to recreate some of these long-lost but important rituals.

Another joyful culinary ritual that has virtually disappeared is the idea of leftovers. With food no longer given the status it deserves, and the whole concept of eating demoted to the idea that it is something we do in between the important things in life, the pace and style of eating have changed. There was a time, though, when the culinary high spot of the week was the Sunday dinner. It is regrettable that we have made our lives so busy that we no longer have a day of rest. To my mind, it is a tradition worth reviving. In the same way that the cycle of the seasons imparts a satisfying rhythm to life, so the shorter frequency of the weekly meal cycle underscores the main rhythm, culminating with the Sunday joint.

The sense of anticipation for that special meal on Sunday bestowed a sense of occasion. It may have been only one meal in the week, but it gave structure to family life. As the centrepiece of a key family gathering, the Sunday roast was meat or poultry at its best, hot and sizzling from the oven and traditionally carved at the table. Though modern man might think this kind of quaint custom risible in this new world of ours, its disappearance is a social loss, as the whole day was about relaxation, communal interaction and the strength of the family.

With more than enough to eat on Sunday, there would be something left over. I remember as a child looking forward to bubble-and-squeak, because there was a certain succulence about leftover vegetables being fried up the next day. Some little bit of culinary alchemy took place when the potatoes browned and crisped in the pan. When there was enough gravy left from the roast, we would have it re-heated and poured over slices of cold meat and the fried vegetables, and sometimes the gravy would be added to the vegetables as they cooked, creating a moist aromatic hash. What a sad world it has become in which we can now buy frozen bubble-and-squeak in the supermarket. Have we really made ourselves that busy that we can no longer spend the time in the kitchen creating our own bubble-and-squeak?

I am all for the idea of leftovers, and the concept of simple meals through the week building up again to the meal of the week on Sunday.

To work with more humble ingredients during the week is to become inventive. To be inventive whilst cooking is to experience joy, especially when that inventiveness conjures up another meal out of nowhere and is rewarded with clean plates and sighs of contentment at the end of a simple repast. At Aspen House, we often prepare buckwheat as a Polish-style kasha, which we have with brisket of beef cooked to one of my Mum's recipes. Fresh from the oven, the beef is wonderfully tasty, but the leftover version the next day is a new dish in its own right. Mixing kasha, gravy and some diced slow-roasted brisket makes a heavenly meaty risotto that is so flavoursome and moreish that it is truly a major disappointment when it has all gone. The joy of revamping the leftovers from a previous meal is not to be underestimated. It is something to be encouraged, even though it is something that today might have to be taught from scratch. Now, there is an opportunity for an enterprising cookery school – showing people how to live well without spending loads of money.

Chicken tonight?

Forget the bottled sauces, and forget the industrial chicken. Try something really different tonight, a real outdoor naturally fed bird. Yes, it will cost you more, but it will taste superb, it will do you good and you can make it go a long way.

Firstly, let's go for the roast. It is this easy. Pick a bird around 2kg in weight, put a few sprigs of fresh herbs (rosemary, thyme, marjoram) two quarters of lemon and two cloves of garlic inside the bird, then smear the breast and legs all over with butter. Sprinkle a couple of glugs of olive oil in a roasting pan, put the chicken in and place it in the oven at 220°C for 15 minutes, to start to crisp up the skin and seal in the juices. After 15 minutes, turn the oven down to 190°C and cook for another 45 minutes.

At this point it will be just cooked through. Remove the herbs, lemon and garlic from inside the chicken and add them to the pan juices, then transfer it to a plate to keep warm. Let it rest for 15 minutes or so while you make the gravy. Add a cup of boiling water to the roasting pan to make it easy to scrape all the sticky bits off the bottom. Tip everything into a small saucepan, including what was inside the bird and simmer it for ten minutes to extract maximum flavour. Strain the liquid into another pan and discard the bits of herb, etc. Thicken the liquid with a teaspoon of cornflour dissolved in a little water, then season to taste with sea salt and black pepper. For a richer gravy, mix a couple of dessertspoons of crème fraiche and Dijon mustard and stir this into the gravy while it is off the heat.

A chicken of this size should feed 4-6 people, but remember to save the bones for stock. What meat you have left, depending on the number of people, can be used for a meal the next day, either in a stir-fry, a salad, a rice dish or whatever takes your fancy. When you have stripped the carcase, put the bones in a pot with a small onion, a carrot, a couple of sticks of celery, a bay leaf and any other herbs you may have. Cover with water, bring to the boil and simmer for about an hour, then strain the liquid off and discard the bones and vegetables. The stock will still be cloudy but can be used just as it is for soups or gravies.

If you want to clarify it, you will need the stock to be cool, and you will need two egg whites beaten but not too stiff. Put the stock into a saucepan and turn the heat to medium. Float the beaten egg whites on top and, as the stock is heating, gradually stir the whites in. As the soup approaches boiling point, with you stirring all the while, the whites will begin to absorb the particles in the stock until they are all gone. By this time the stock will be at boiling point and the egg whites will have turned into something quite unappetising. Strain the liquid through muslin to catch the solids, which can then be discarded. The stock at this point should be completely clear. If you are not going to use it immediately, it will freeze very well and last for at least six months.

It is not difficult to philosophise on the joy of food, or indeed the joy of life itself, for is it not true that happiness is a goal worth aiming for? I could cover many pages talking about what makes us happy, what doesn't and how the concept of happiness has been altered to suit the adman's brief, but it's all been said. What is not said so often is that happiness is fundamental and comes from within – it cannot be bought. It is up to each of us to work towards whatever constitutes our own personal state of contentment. What I can add to the discussion is my own discovery that food is the place to start. Revive the joy of eating and you have the basis for continued happiness right there. The enjoyment of food, and an understanding of how this creates a bedrock for a cheerful outlook on life, is perhaps the key to our salvation. At the very least, eating joyfully means that a sizeable proportion of our waking hours will be spent being happy. From there, the only way is up.

There is a story I once heard, which you may well have heard too, for it no doubt forms the stuff of fable. The story concerns a man who lives on what might be described as a paradise island. He lives there with his wife and his children as part of a community of happy islanders. Each day, he spends some time with his family, playing with his children and attending to the little everyday jobs that help to keep everything running smoothly. Then he goes off down to the beach for a spot of fishing. He likes fishing and devotes much of his time to this favourite distraction.

One day another man comes ashore in a big boat. This man is dressed in strange clothes, what we might call a business suit. He carries papers and a pen. He comes to speak to the islander, and tells him that he is sitting on a great fortune, for under the ground of this tiny island lie deposits of crude oil and minerals. He tells the islander that there are other men across the ocean who would pay big money for the rights to drill and mine on the island.

"I have no use for money," says the islander.

"But money will buy you things," says the businessman, extending his arms, "Lots of things, and you will become rich. And when you are rich, you will be able to go to other islands just like this one and you will be able to use your riches to buy the rights to drill on those other islands too, and you will become even richer still."

"And what will I do with all these riches?" asks the islander.

"Well, that's the point," says the businessman excitedly, "You won't have to do anything. Your money will buy you all the time in the world, and you'll be able to do anything you like. If you wanted to, you could even go fishing all day!"

"But that's what I do now," says the islander.

For far too long we have listened to the voices of those men in strange clothes, with their paper and pens and their ideas about wealth and money. The truth is that Earth is our paradise island, and if we had maintained a healthy relationship with the Earth we might still be spending time with our family and friends, playing with our children and doing the odd bit of essential work, leaving time to go fishing every day. Look at our Earth, our paradise island floating in the sea of space. It is the only island we have, the only place we have in which to live. It surely must be time to clean it up and make it a fit place to live in once again.

And how can we do that? The task is not easy, but not impossible. It seems to me that food is the starting point. Turning our backs on the idea of industrialised food in favour of real food points us easily in one direction only, and that is the ultimate localisation of our food supply, for how else can we reclaim our agricultural land from the grip of industrialisation? How else can we guarantee that the food we eat is fresh, seasonal and uncontaminated by any chemical inputs? The only way we can do it is to grow the food ourselves or, if we cannot do that, to deal directly with those who do grow food, for in that direct relationship, as part of a local community, is bred trust. Once links start to appear in the chain and it goes outside of our immediate neighbourhood, the bond is weakened, the trust diluted. We need that trust undiluted. In that trust lies joy, the joy that comes from understanding the essence of growing, cooking and eating food, and from knowing that we are not being conned by those who provide the food for us. Generally, we have to eat something every few hours merely to stay alive. Removing joy from this experience diminishes our lives, but each one of us has the means to recover the situation. Changing as quickly or as slowly as each of us can manage, we can transform the way we see our food and transform the land that grows it, bringing back health to land, plants, animals and us. Therein lies true joy.

> *"One of the very nicest things about life is the way we must regularly stop whatever it is we are doing and devote our attention to eating."*
> Luciano Pavarotti and William Wright, Pavarotti,
> My Own Story

Chapter Seven

Eat . . . locally

In Littledean in the Forest of Dean, not far from where my grandfather used to farm, there is a memorial. It is not the usual stone cross commemorating the fallen of two World Wars, yet it is a memorial as poignant as any I have seen.

Nothing more than a stone-slabbed platform built from the local sandstone, it is reminiscent of the platforms on which dairy farmers, before the days of bulk tankers, would leave their milk churns to be collected each morning, and indeed there are milk churns on this plinth today. A slate plaque built into its side carries a simple message: *Dedicated to all the dairymen who once farmed in this parish.* There is something deeply sad about the fact that the residents of Littledean feel sufficiently moved to commemorate the loss of rural livelihood in this way. For them, the loss is obviously no less profound than that precipitated by the local boys dying in some senseless war.

Not five miles away from Littledean is one of the last of the traditional dairymen of the Forest of Dean, and the man from whom we now get our unpasteurised real milk. On the verge of retirement, with a son and daughter who have already moved into different occupations because of the insanity of trying to run a small traditional dairy herd in a world of global competition, this farmer is the only one in

Gloucestershire still supplying real milk. There is a double tragedy here. Firstly, our farming heritage has been allowed to slip into oblivion by a succession of misguided, or possibly incompetent, governments and agricultural policies that favour the land barons. Secondly, our choice as consumers has been taken from us, and only a few of us are now in the position of being able to choose unpasteurised milk, if that is what we wish to drink.

Most of us are drinking standardised, homogenised, pasteurised milk with the cream removed. Sold to us on a health ticket (semi-skimmed milk = low fat = good for your heart) this commodity milk is virtually a non-food. Pasteurisation kills good bacteria as well as bad, and it destroys the enzymes that enable us to digest lactose and absorb the calcium in the milk. Homogenisation breaks down the fat into such small globules that the body can no longer effectively digest it, and thus it becomes harmful. On top of it all, commodity milk comes from dairy cows that are fed an unnatural protein-rich diet and overworked to the point of sickness and early death. The products of such an industry should carry a government health warning, yet it is the unpasteurised milk that we are warned against – another example of our topsy-turvy wonderland. And once our small pasture-fed traditional herds have gone, they are gone for good.

> *"He who pasteurises good milk is a fool, and he who pasteurises bad milk is a rogue."*
> Cmdr Geoffrey Bowles RN July 1943

Recently, we met someone called Alan who once used to be a dairy farmer. He kept twenty-odd head of Jersey cows on the rich pastures of Howle Hill near Ross-on-Wye. He was one of over twenty dairy farmers who prospered in that area and, from his small operation, he could make a decent living. Every December, he would supplement his income by selling around 15 cockerels to grace the Christmas dinner tables of those who fancied something other than goose, turkey or beef. Cockerel really was a special treat, and each one could be sold at a good price – a useful Christmas bonus for this particular dairyman.

But that was a long time ago. All of those diary farmers have now gone, driven to the wall by ruinous price fixing at the hands of Government legislation, agri-business and the supermarkets.

"The supermarkets have killed it," says Alan, "No one can make a living any more. If you don't accept the price you are being offered, the big boys just go somewhere else. They buy on the world market."

This story is repeated by those we know who are still in farming, but who have had to diversify in order to keep their way of life.

"There were once twenty-five dairymen in this valley," another farmer, Duncan, tells us, "Now there is only one."

Farming in the beautifully undulating countryside around the village of Woolhope, a picturesque backwater of Herefordshire ideally suited to traditional mixed farming, Duncan has memories of how his farm thrived two generations ago, and how the rich land would yield an abundance rarely seen today. In the face of crippling price impositions by the all-powerful retailers, Duncan and his wife, Gail, have reinstated the viability of the farm by getting out of the madness of trying to compete in a world market. By diversifying into the growing of vegetables, they can operate in the local market via their own organic box scheme, supplementing their customers' choice with their own impressive selection of home baked artisan bread.

Forget global – think local

Duncan and Gail Sayce, from Woolhope, could so easily have become one more statistic in the sad story of British farming, but they opted out of the system and took a chance on becoming local suppliers, first through growing and selling their own organic vegetables via their own veg box scheme, Shared Harvest, and then by specialising in artisan breadmaking, which now includes running courses for aspiring bakers.

Shared Harvest is not only successful but it breaks new ground. In their own fields, Duncan grows the organic wheat, spelt and rye that they use to make their bread, and they mill it themselves, making fresh flour for each new batch of bread. This truly is baking at its best. Freshly milled flour has a gorgeous sweet and nutty aroma that translates into loaves of exceptional fragrance and high nutritional value.

We think Duncan and Gail are showing us the way to our future on this Earth. Globalisation has wrecked the planet, but localisation might just save it and, at the same time, it enables us to reclaim the right to eat wholesome nutritious food.

"My granddad used to keep three thousand chickens, not in prison sheds but running around these fields, and he even grew wild mushrooms," Duncan relates, "He used to put them on the train to Birmingham and, one year, he made enough profit on the mushrooms to buy two new cars and a new tractor."

Apparently, Duncan's grandfather knew how to bring the mushrooms on with the right combination of composts and seaweed culture. At the right time of year, he could turn his pastures white with wild field mushrooms. Picked by a workforce of local women prepared to labour in the fields from the early hours ensured that the mushrooms were boxed up and on the Birmingham train to be sold to the market traders. Real wild field mushrooms from the green fields of Herefordshire.

Now it's all changed.

At the time of writing, dairy farmers around Herefordshire and the Welsh Borders, keeping cattle on some of the finest pastureland in the country, are being offered 26p per litre for milk that costs them 30p a litre to produce. It does not take an accountant to see that this is the road to bankruptcy. And, as we saw in Chapter Four, those who shop in supermarkets are contributing to the problem by unwittingly endorsing it. Though it comes as a shock when thought of in these terms, each one of us who buys milk off the supermarket shelf is unconsciously taking from our farmers the opportunity to make a viable living and thereby contributing to the loss of their living and the even more serious loss of our farming heritage.

To illustrate what powerful forces we and those poor farmers are up against, let's look at one of the largest supermarkets in this country in the run-up to Christmas. In contrast to Alan making a small Christmas bonus by selling fifteen cockerels to people in his own community, Asda expect to distribute around 9.5 million turkeys nationwide through its stores in the two weeks before Christmas. In an act easily interpreted as a body blow to small farmers, Alan's small-time cockerel operation was stopped many years ago after an EU directive shut down most of this country's small abattoirs. Alan was told that he would no longer be allowed to sell cockerels because his volume was too small and he was too far from the nearest slaughterhouse.

In that other world, that world where subsidies favour the larger operators, the big retailers have grown unchecked, putting all but the biggest and most ruthless farming operations out of business. In two generations, we have lost around 70% of our small farms. As the absolute antithesis of community shopping (despite all their protestations to the contrary), the supermarkets are now so gargantuan they are frightening. Going back to the Asda example, there was a brief video clip shown on the BBC website in December 2008, telling us how Asda plans for Christmas. The planning starts just as soon as the previous Christmas is over, giving Asda a whole year to work out what and how much will sell. They will even look at the last time Christmas fell on the same day of the week, take into account how much the business has grown since then and, using the latest sophisticated forecast technology, work out, line by line, item by item, exactly how much they will sell next Christmas.

Leading up to Christmas 2008, the depot at Wakefield in Yorkshire, one of 25 depots around the country, handled 900 trucks every 24 hours on a round-the-clock 7-day a week operation. Nearly one thousand workers ensured that the Wakefield depot delivered on time to all of the stores it services. It was a similar scenario at each of the other depots, with each one delivering to about forty or fifty stores via an average of 25 trucks per day for each store. In the gigantic warehouses, the picking for the store deliveries is computer-controlled. Instructions go directly to the fork-lift operators via a headset, giving the operator precise orders based on what was sold in any given store on the previous day, or even that morning in the case of afternoon deliveries.

What is most depressing about this is the sheer cold-eyed efficiency of it all. There is something disturbing about the ruthless predictability of sales and profits. These giant retailers are often heard to criticise their High Street counterparts by saying that, if they want to stay in business, they should get more efficient and more competitive, but no one-man operation can compete with the might of these retail behemoths. Every hour of every day, they roll on regardless, crushing all in their path. They will do whatever they have to do to keep that balance sheet looking healthy, to keep their shareholders sweet and to keep their competitors away from them.

This kind of business is no good for either the local economy or the local community. Big business sucks money out of both like a stealthy vampire. The profit made by these huge corporations leaves town and finds its way into the pockets of high-ranking executives and delighted shareholders. The profit made by a local grocer will most likely be spent within the same community, where the money will go around again and again. For this reason, if for no other, making a personal choice to shop locally, and support independent traders rather than any High Street multi-nationals, brings wealth and prosperity to towns and communities.

"If fresh food is necessary to health in man and beast, then that food must be provided not only from our own soil but as near as possible to the sources of consumption. If this involves fewer imports and consequent repercussions on exports then it is industry that must be readjusted to the needs of food. If such readjustment involves the decentralisation of industry and the re-opening of local mills and slaughterhouses, then the health of the nation is more important than any large combine."
Lady Eve Balfour, Founder of the Soil Association, 1943

The concept of 'local' has succumbed to the blowtorch of the inaptly named Green Revolution, when chemical farming got under way in earnest after World War II. The Agriculture Act of 1947 actually made it illegal for any small farmer to defy the Government, on pain of having his land confiscated as a penalty for wishing to remain organic. That was the beginning of the end for traditional farming, and from the ashes of that noble heritage grew the dark phoenix of what is absurdly called conventional farming. There is nothing conventional about a system which has been in place for less than a century, not when one considers that, in Asia and the Far East, farmers have worked the land continuously for forty centuries without diminishing its fertility and without using chemical fertilisers or pesticides.

Our Western 'conventional' farming, coming into its own only in the second half of the 20ᵗʰ Century, has managed virtually to destroy the major part of our fertile farmland, killing not only whole ecological systems of microbial life within the soil, but also the small birds and animals that were once dependent on it. The humus and organic material which binds soil and gives it life have been quickly and efficiently removed over a few short decades of intensive chemical farming. Small farms raising animals for food and growing a variety of crops to supply local communities have been crushed by the juggernaut of subsidy-supported cash crop agri-business, whose monoculture mania has quite simply robbed us all of the opportunity to eat healthy nutritional food. Those millions of acres of commodity crops are inextricably tied in with the food processing industry. Their factories turn out nutritionally depleted products by the billion, sold to us through blatantly disingenuous claims that they are more healthy than the real foods once grown on those same fields when my granddad was still farming. To illustrate the size of these operations, it is worth thinking about this for a moment: Premier Foods, the UK's largest 'food' manufacturer, owning brands like Hovis, Homepride, Mr Kipling, Branstons, Sharwoods, Angel Delight etc., takes *8.5% of the UK's wheat crop* into its factories. In terms of the acreage required to produce such a quantity, this is the equivalent of the entire land mass of Bedfordshire, Buckinghamshire, Northamptonshire and Oxfordshire put together. And it is all being turned into useless artificial foods. That, to my mind at least, is truly scary.

Mushroom and Cheese Special

Some people call this French Toast, whilst the French themselves might call it pain perdu. More popularly, it goes by the name of 'eggy bread.' The version we do might well be called mozzarella in carrozza in Italy, but we just call it our Mushroom and Cheese Special. All suggestions for something snappier are most welcome.

For each sandwich, you will need:
bread, butter and cheese
one large egg (or 2 medium)
4-5 young button mushrooms
some butter/olive oil for frying
1tbs crème fraiche
salt and pepper
1tsp chopped parsley, chives or lovage (or all three!)

We like to make this with local artisan cheese, and we find that Little Hereford from Monkland Dairy works really well. Plus it comes complete with an intriguing story, so that adds charm as well as taste. Mark and Karen Hindle, proprietors of the dairy as well as several retail outlets that go by the name of Mousetrap Cheese, discovered the recipe for Little Hereford, written up in 1918 by one Ellen Yeld, 'Chief Dairy Instructress under the Herefordshire County Council.' It's a great cheese, so the recipe was worth resurrecting, in our opinion.

When mushrooms are in season, that's an added bonus, but we are lucky enough to be able to get commercially produced organic brown chestnut mushrooms from Whitethorn Farm, so we usually use these. We use our own home baked bread and eggs from one of our local suppliers. The crème fraiche we use comes from Bower Farm, just over the border into Wales, but it is delivered to our local farm shop.

Start this off by making a cheese sandwich. Then cut off the crusts, creating a square, before cutting it diagonally into two triangles. In a shallow bowl, beat up the egg seasoned with sea salt and black pepper, then pop in the two triangles of cheese sandwich and leave them long enough to absorb the egg thoroughly on both sides.

Meanwhile, slice the mushrooms and fry them gently in a little butter until completely wilted. Season lightly with salt and pepper, then stir in the crème fraiche and stir fry for a few minutes until the cream thickens. Take it off the heat, stir in the chopped herbs and set aside in a warm oven while you fry the sandwich gently on both sides in a little butter and olive oil. When the sandwich is cooked through (a couple of minutes each side) the cheese in the middle will have melted.

Place the triangles of fried sandwich on a plate and spoon over the creamy mushrooms. Enjoy.

As I write, a crop sprayer drives down the road outside our house. It is the sixth that has driven past in the last three days – just on one road in one village. The same thing is happening all over the county, all over the UK, all over Europe, the USA and the rest of the developed world. Come harvest time for cereal crops, we will see gigantic combines bully their way down these narrow lanes like bouncers on their way to a midnight rave. They are too big for such roads, but the huge fields of cereals demand huge harvesters to reap them. Once harvested, the fields will be immediately replanted with the next cash crop – time is money, and there is no concern for the condition of the soil when artificial fertilisers are available to bring the crops on. Granted, they might fall over because they are growing too quickly, or they might succumb to disease and predation because they have no integral cell strength, but that is what all those fungicides, insecticides and herbicides are for, so no worries there. The new chemical rulebook merely instructs the 'farmer' to douse the crop with as many chemicals as it takes to keep it going until harvest time. And if all that wheat, already adulterated to the point of toxicity by its diet of noxious chemicals, then has any remaining life crushed out of it by gigantic industrial roller mills, it is of no concern to the person who grows it. A grower is simply concerned with selling the crop for the right price. Everything else is someone else's problem. In any case, no one will know that the bleached white powdered carbohydrate, now masquerading as flour, is injurious to health. After all, it looks very clean, so it must be healthy, whether it comes in its basic form as flour or as the ubiquitous white sliced loaf that sells as the nation's favourite loss leader in every supermarket in the land.

Intensive farming is about money. It is about a global food industry, about economies of scale and the protection under the World Trade Organisation, whose original manifesto is unrecognisable in the 'free trade' principles it now employs to protect the biggest growers on the planet and push the smallest out of existence. The progress of the global food industry is relentless. Though it has been demonstrated time and time again right through the 20th Century that intensive agriculture is an unsustainable short-term enterprise, the big players now seem too powerful to stop. Thus the ruination of the world's fertile land resources is likely to continue until the process reaches its logical and inevitable conclusion. Meanwhile, the ethics of animal husbandry too have all but disappeared. Every day of every year, countless millions of living creatures – cattle, pigs, dairy cows and poultry – are subjected to appalling brutality in the industry's desire to treat these sentient beings as mere commodities.

Such callousness is deeply offensive, yet, like so much unacceptable human behaviour before it, for example, the persecution of Jews down the centuries, it is easy to justify, but not so easy to defend. To paraphrase Shylock, Shakespeare's immortal Jew, are not all living creatures 'warmed and cooled by the same winter and summer' as we are? Sadly, no. Many are not. Domesticated farm animals are increasingly confined in cruelly cramped indoor conditions, prevented from indulging in natural behaviour and never allowed to see the light of day. And, as with Shylock, when you prick them, they certainly bleed. A tiny piglet subjected to castration or tail-docking squeals in real pain, while its mother, penned in a sow stall for up to five years of constant breeding, has the same look of abject sadness as any prisoner in the stinking cells of dictatorial regimes. Intensive animal production is just another of those regimes, and we blindly buy into it by accepting the products of factory farming.

More sinister still is the rise of genetically modified (GM) crops. The arguments in favour of GM agriculture remain unconvincing, yet the most powerful corporations on the planet, with lobbying control over weakened and corrupt governments, insist that GM will save the world. It will do nothing of the sort. It will merely make companies like Monsanto, Syngenta and Bayer even richer than they are at present, ultimately giving them control over what seeds can be planted, when and where. It is clear that, in their quest for an ever more profitable bottom line, these companies wish to patent life itself.

Though the subject of GM and the science behind it are both very complex, the dangers are simple to see. It can be said quite logically that the hazards of working in what amounts to a fundamentally unnatural fashion could threaten the collapse of complete ecosystems. The truth is that we really do not know what we are unleashing. Genetic Modification is not simply a variation on the kind of breeding techniques that have been practiced by farmers and seedsmen for centuries. This is something completely different, something that can throw up very unpredictable results. Surely it is clear that a plant containing a fish gene is not in its natural state, nor could it ever survive such a genetic crossover without the intervention of some outside agency. In the long term (something corporations like Monsanto seem to disregard) there is no telling what poisons or other toxins might be released by a plant with fish genes it its sap.

Intense lobbying by the leading GM companies has ensured that only the bare minimum of testing has been carried out on the effects of GM tinkering in plant hybrids, so we really have no definite idea of the long term effects on human health of consuming such plants. Yet, the US soya, wheat and maize crops are already awash with genetically modified strains, many of which find their way into food products from the big manufacturers. Do we know for sure that processed foods, such as breakfast cereals, soft drinks, flour-based products (including those food products coated in batter, such as chicken nuggets or fish fillets) and anything containing soya or maize derivatives, are free from GM contamination? The simple truth is that we don't. In addition, most processed foods contain one or more of the above-mentioned derivatives, for example, soya lechitin, modified corn starch, mono-, di- and triglycerides of fatty acids, maltodextrin, maltose, high fructose corn syrup (HFCS), xanthan gum and even ascorbic or citric acid. There are some 12,000 food products currently stocked on supermarket shelves that contain some kind of maize or soya derivative – and it doesn't stop there. These chemical additives also appear in the waxy shine on supermarket cucumbers, apples and other fruit, and even in toothpaste and other non-food items. For more information on GM, have a look at www.gmfreeze.org

Another voice unheard . . . when will we start to listen?

"Now I truly believe that we in this generation must come to terms with nature, and I think we're challenged, as mankind has never been challenged before, to prove our maturity and our mastery, not of nature but of ourselves."
Rachel Carson [1907 – 1962]

I hope the picture I am painting is clear enough without having to labour the point. Essentially, the staggering rise in intensive farming practices since the end of World War II has led us into all sorts of mischief, as the thirst for corporate profit outweighed moral, ethical, ecological and humanitarian principles. To put it another way, Sir Walter Scott's words seem quite apt in this context: "Oh what a tangled web we weave, When first we practice to deceive!" And deceived we are, for so many of these modern processed foods, grown on degraded soils and contaminated with toxic inputs, are sold to us with a health label firmly stuck to the packaging.

The one thought that makes this depressing scenario bearable is that we have the power to change it. It is our money that buys what these corporations want to sell us, and they are powerful only because we part with our money, directly or indirectly, to purchase the products they sell. This is their Achilles' heel. The money is their lifeblood. If we withdraw our support, we turn off the supply. Even the biggest companies quickly become vulnerable if their source of profitability is removed. By making the decision that we are not prepared to buy what they are offering, we are voting for a better way of life, a better way of eating, and we can build on that by opting to source our food locally, direct from the producer, from an independent trader such as a farm shop, or even directly from our own back gardens.

In the foregoing chapters, I trust I have managed to convey something of how bleak a future lies in a continued reliance on industrial food. My wish is to illustrate the difference between real food and its industrial mimic and to provide sufficient motivation for change. If we know what we are looking at when faced with today's bewildering abundance of foodstuffs, then we are empowered with knowledge and can make informed choices about what we eat. Thus, for instance, if we go into our local farm shop and we see out-of-season vegetables, we will know that we are looking at imported produce. Around Ross-on-Wye, our local town, it is possible to see bags of 'local' potatoes for sale in filling stations and corner shops, but the name on the bag gives the game away. The potatoes come from the intensive fields of one of the big growers in the county, and so are tainted with chemicals. Buying from Martin and Rachel at Carey Organics, by contrast, guarantees quality, because you are dealing directly with the person who grows them.

Assuming that we are aiming to buy fresh food in season, two caveats should influence our buying decisions, even from a local independent shop. Firstly, we should ask ourselves how long is the chain between us and the grower. If it is more than two links long, there is a danger that we will lose the trail of provenance. Secondly, size matters. A local producer can work to his own personal vision when below a certain size, but beyond that point will be subject to economic and financial constraints that change the nature of the operation and could easily compromise the quality of the product. So, if a company begins to grow, beware. If ever there was a case for thinking 'small is beautiful,' the sourcing of our food is it. Remember that the whole point of sourcing food locally is that this is the only guaranteed way of buying fresh, seasonal, uncontaminated real food, with the feel-good bonus of knowing that, by shopping like this, we are all helping to reverse the suicidal dead end thinking of the industrial food system.

Chapter eight

Eat . . . simply

Just before Christmas 2004, we treated ourselves to a short break in Copenhagen. It was like discovering a portal between two parallel universes. The world we left was one in which Roy Wood and Wizard, bellowing a death wish for it to be Christmas every day, dominated the music systems of practically every trashy coruscating High Street shop, as eddies of blank-eyed and directionless lost souls drifted around, parting with money that wasn't theirs in exchange for seasonal junk they didn't need.

The world on the other side of the portal was clean, calm and civilised, full of elegance and an implicit air of quiet grace, despite the fact that Copenhagen is a busy and prosperous modern city. Tradition and an unspoken assumption that human values are still important make this city an exemplar of urban living.

No visit to Copenhagen at Christmas would be complete without a visit to the magnificent 160-year old Tivoli Gardens, with its faded but stubbornly resplendent charm. Defiant in its waning yet timeless looks, it holds its own like some triumphant grand dame, some glorious diva with a golden past, and continues to delight the senses despite its age. To pass through the entrance turnstiles is literally to step back in time. Everything takes on a different air, and the whole place feels like a gigantic time machine. As we wandered through this sparkling winter playground, we felt the sense of a more genteel past in which life was slower and much simpler than today. Nowhere did we feel this more acutely than when we came upon a street vendor selling fast food.

Not for him the mass-market toxic burgers of every fairground in England. Not for him the awful re-hydrated onions bought by the sack from a warehouse cash & carry. This man was a master of his craft, and offering a different take on the widely popular Danish hot-dog. Instead of the more usual sausage and onion wrapped in bread, this vendor was frying sliced potatoes and onions along with chunks of Danish sausage. There is much to choose from in Tivoli Gardens, from a Michelin-starred restaurant to a take-away pizza stall, but there was nothing to beat the aroma of what was sizzling in this man's enormous pan. The secret of his success was quite possibly the onions, as there is nothing like a waft of fried onions to make people say, "Gosh! That smells good – what's cooking?" It happens at Aspen House on a regular basis, and indeed the onion is an essential ingredient if you want simple cooking to be touched by the magic wand of alchemy. And alchemy it was that took place that night in the Tivoli Gardens. For us, on a crisp December night in that magical romantic spot, surrounded by thousands of twinkling lights, this was the meal of the century – a simple plate of fried potatoes, onion and continental sausage. Not solely because of the atmosphere and the fact that we were on holiday, but because this street vendor had gone to the trouble of cooking not just fast food but real food. Simple, satisfying and so tasty. Since then, his succulent dish has become a favourite of ours, and it features quite frequently on our personal winter menu.

Some would argue that this sort of food is no more than ordinary rustic fare. I couldn't agree more, and that is what makes it so appealing. The fancy creations of TV chefs, with their jellies, foams, dollops, blobs and smears, occupy a certain segment of the culinary arts, but all food shares the same pedigree, and that goes back to what was cooked in the rustic peasant homes of traditional cultures. Just look at some of the classic books on the subject of simple food and you will easily see there the roots of even the fanciest dishes. In seeking ideas that appeal to the palate as well as to the eye, we need look no further than Elizabeth Luard's *The Rich Tradition of European Peasant Cookery*, or Elizabeth David's *Book of Mediterranean Food* and Jane Grigson's *Vegetable Book*. All classics of their time, books like these are precious storehouses of culinary ideas. Just thumbing through *The Rich Tradition*, for instance, is a mouth-watering experience, especially as the recipes therein are eminently do-able. Fussy food has its place, but simple food hits the spot. It is within the reach of even those with limited experience in the kitchen and is guaranteed to earn brownie points at the dinner table.

This essence of culinary success is the maxim by which we try to operate at Aspen House: simple but effective. We prepare food for guests who are paying for the privilege of eating it, so we do take care with what we cook, how we cook it and how we present it. Certain guests would be more than happy to tuck into a Tivoli fry-up, if that is what we were cooking that night but, if we were to serve such a dish, we would make certain that it was presented in a visually appealing way. For us, this is all you need – uncomplicated, but fresh and seasonal ingredients prepared in a simple way that lets them speak for themselves, and presented to look good on the plate.

Aspen House Tivoli fry-up

Every culinary heritage has at least one dish that is based on what has become a classic combination of potatoes and onions, some with the optional extras of cheese and/or meat. From hash browns to Swiss rösti, and from the French Pommes Boulangère to our very own Northumbrian Pan Haggerty, the taste of potato and onion together is so universal as to be seen as indispensable for any cook wishing to satisfy a diner's hunger.

Sally and I have come up with our own version of this winning combination, based on our trip to Tivoli Gardens. For the two of us, we use around one pound (500 grams) of floury potatoes, two medium sized English onions (avoid the big Spanish ones –

too bland), four slices of bacon and any other bits that come to hand, such as breakfast sausages or black pudding. For the frying medium, we tend to alternate between goose fat or olive oil with butter, though the latter probably makes for a more interesting final flavour. Just to give the whole thing a touch of the Wow Factor, we also have some grated cheese handy, preferably something like Montgomery Cheddar.

The method is foolproof. Peel and slice the potatoes and parboil them, drain and dry them off by shaking the pot containing them over the heat until any remaining moisture evaporates. Heat the oil in a good non-stick pan and add the potatoes, turning them to coat them in the oil. Season with salt and pepper and let them cook on medium heat to brown them slowly while you deal with the rest.

Heat up a good splash of olive oil (or bacon fat, if you have some) in another pan. Take the skins off the onions, cut them in half top to bottom and cut each half into slices. Remove the rind from the bacon, cut the slices into ½ inch strips and fry gently until cooked. Do the same with the sausages and black pudding, if you are using them. Once cooked, set all these aside and fry the onions gently in the same pan, mostly with the lid on, because this helps to keep them moist while they brown slightly on the bottom.

When the onions are turning to golden brown, add the bacon, etc and stir it through to keep it warm. As soon as the potatoes are browned to your liking, tip in the contents of the other pan and mix thoroughly, then sprinkle a few handfuls of grated cheese on top, put on the lid and leave the whole thing on low heat for 10 minutes to give the cheese a chance to melt into the contents of the pan. Then you are ready to eat.

By the time you have polished off what's in the pan, you will wonder why you didn't double the quantity.

How refreshing it is to see others subscribing to the same philosophy, more particularly when they are also running a business. In 2008, two young sisters opened a little eatery in Ledbury called Cameron & Swan, which is such a top class place that we now devote time to finding a 'good reason to go to Ledbury'. Hannah Cameron and Bec Swan were brought up on a local family smallholding where the focus was on self-sufficiency long before that became a trendy phrase. Growing their own vegetables and cooking from scratch came naturally to the Camerons, and the family grew up with a respect for the simple pleasures of growing, cooking and eating.

With food being the central focus it should be, it is perhaps no surprise that the two sisters opted for careers in food.

Bec completed a year's training at Leith's School of Food and Wine, and went on to a glittering career, travelling all over Europe cooking for many high-profile celebrities and VIPs. Hannah, meanwhile, having graduated from university, left for London, where initially she managed a deli in Clapham before moving on to living the glamorous life of working on the food section of a glossy magazine. Yet the simple life was ultimately a bigger pull and, despite the kind of high rolling lifestyles that many people can only dream of, both Hannah and Bec were drawn back to Herefordshire.

With Bec now married, she and Hannah still hankered for an occupation that would continue to keep them in touch with food. As is often the way with such ideas, the right premises came up at the right time and, after much planning, Cameron & Swan was born, a new uniquely individual eatery imbued from its opening day with the personalities of its owners. How very intimate it is to enjoy a coffee and a scone in the window seat and gaze at the old family photographs on the wall of the two sisters helping their mother in the kitchen when they were just little girls. A world away from all those cloned and impersonal themed coffee houses that have spread insidiously through our towns.

From the start, Bec and Hannah had certain ideals from which they would not stray. Although Bec was obviously keen to put her culinary skills to good use in the kitchen, preparing excellent fresh food to order,

Hannah always imagined that the place could also work as a deli, as well as a showcase for local products they were using in their own kitchen. As a matter of principle, there is nothing used or sold here that is normally available at the supermarket. By sticking to their principles, Bec and Hannah are making a stand for real food. Their shelves are filled with all manner of local artisan products, as is the deli counter.

Above all, their ethos is to serve honest simple food. The kitchen is open-plan, so that anyone who comes in can see Bec busy preparing everything from scratch, and certainly not relying on catering packs and microwaves. Taking their cue from their parents and their grow-your-own practicality, Bec and Hannah do not go to great pains to encumber themselves with labels such as 'organic' or 'fair trade', believing it to be far more powerful to source as directly as they can the best of artisan produce, whether it is bread made by hand at a local bakery or superb British charcuterie made just over the border in Monmouthshire. Some of what they buy, the bread for example, is sourced directly and, where this is not possible, small-scale wholesalers are used. The wonderful selection of wines, for instance, is supplied by an independent wine merchant who runs his business from just a few miles away. By working like this, and reducing the number of middlemen to a minimum whilst dealing with producers who share the same world view, terms like 'organic' and 'fair trade' are implicit.

As to the food itself, the emphasis is on simplicity or, as Hannah puts it, "Honest, seasonal food, simply prepared and presented well." That is exactly what you get, whether it is a coffee and a slice of home made cake or one of the excellent light lunches on offer on the blackboard that dominates one wall. What more do we require of food than this? There is no need to dress food up in fancy trimmings. By using fresh ingredients in season, it would be sacrilegious not to allow those ingredients to speak for themselves, and the food at Cameron & Swan does just that. More importantly, by keeping it simple, Bec and Hannah are showing us the essential nature of food, the hub of all things. By eating at a place like Cameron & Swan, we hope that their customers are saying, "Yes, food does matter. Yes, eating fresh seasonal food prepared for us by someone who cares is a more human experience than eating the processed equivalent in a production line coffee house and, yes, places like this represent our future."

It is my firm belief that part of what we need to do to revive our relationship with food is to support local businesses like Cameron & Swan. In other words, we should support those who support local producers and work within the radius of their own community. By doing so, we create a virtuous circle, strengthening our local ties, our community identity and our resilience to any future food crisis. Without wishing to sound political, it is also my belief that we should simply boycott any eateries that are not run by locals using local suppliers.

Cameron & Swan's carrot cake

Bec has very kindly allowed us to publish her recipe for the delicious carrot cake which we always hope will be available when we stop off for a 'little something' on our trips to Ledbury.

Serves 10-12
4 eggs
300ml sunflower oil
350g dark brown sugar
the zest from two oranges
400g self raising flour
4tsp cinnamon
2tsp bicarbonate of soda
400g carrot, peeled and grated
220g chopped pecans
200g sultanas
100g desiccated coconut

For the icing:
250g mascarpone
200g sifted icing sugar

Preheat the oven to 170°C/gas mark 3. Line the base and sides of a 28cm/11" loose bottom cake tin with baking parchment.

In a large mixing bowl whisk by hand the eggs, sunflower oil, sugar and orange zest. Sift the flour, cinnamon and bicarbonate of soda together and add to the egg mixture with the rest of the ingredients. Stir well until combined. Pour this mixture into the prepared cake tin and bake in the middle of the preheated oven for approximately 50 minutes to 1 hour or until a cake tester inserted into the middle of the cake comes out clean. Remove from the oven, leave to cool and then turn out of the tin onto a wire rack.

To make the icing, mix the mascarpone and icing sugar together and beat with an electric hand whisk until combined, then spread over the top of the cake just before serving.

"Truth is ever to be found in simplicity," declared Sir Isaac Newton. Although he was not talking specifically about food, his observation is as applicable to the art of eating as to any other aspect of life. Most of the belief systems that have exhorted us through the ages to seek a path to true happiness focus on simplicity as a key element in this search. My own journey along the path of understanding has led me to a belief in simplicity as a powerful elixir to health and vitality, both physical and spiritual. Simplicity represents true essence, and I see, for instance, the humble hedgerow dog-rose as a more beautiful flower than any multi-petalled ostentatious hybrid. And thus it is with food.

I am not advocating a Spartan diet or the life of an ascetic, because I am not talking about frugality. I am talking about simplicity of cooking and simplicity of presentation. Good food is to be enjoyed for its own tastes and, if the ingredients are real, those tastes will shine through and will not welcome unnecessary embellishments. The concept of 'everything all the time' does nothing to help us understand food and its nourishing qualities, and stacking miles of supermarket shelves with processed products in an endless variety of colourful packaging makes a mockery of the whole idea of food. On top of that, we are presented with a cabaret of TV celebrity chefs who corrupt the art of cooking by turning it into a competition amongst themselves, leaving the viewers feeling thoroughly inadequate. All of this has little to do with the simple acts of growing, cooking and eating real food.

We have seen in earlier chapters what is to be gained from eating naturally, seasonally and sensually. Element by element, like brushing the dust of ages from a long hidden archaeological artefact, we are discovering the fundamental nature of eating. The true spirit of nourishment and the pleasure it brings us is being revealed as an essential part of our human wellbeing. The way we eat reflects the way we are and how we see our relationship with the vastness of Nature, of which we are but a small part. To eat simply is not to stint ourselves or to deprive ourselves of the rich variety of foods available to us. To eat simply is to understand which real foods will nourish us and to have respect for those foods in the way we produce, prepare and present them for consumption.

> *"It may be safely averred that good cookery is the best and truest economy, turning to full account every wholesome article of food, and converting into palatable meals what the ignorant either render uneatable or throw away in disdain."*
> Eliza Acton : Modern Cookery for Private Families (1845)

134

Chapter Nine

Eat . . . communally

On the corner of Mill Street in Hereford is a modest greengrocer's called The Fruit Basket. Until recently, this unassuming little shop was looking a little tired, no doubt worn down through having to survive in a city currently served by nine major supermarket outlets (ten, if you count the M&S food hall). Then one day, along came Teresa Harris, returning to the place of her birth after a decade in London.

Teresa remembered this small shop from her childhood as her local grocery, and felt moved by its air of neglect to regenerate it to serve the community once again. Right on the edge of St James and Bartonsham, a relatively vibrant community-minded district of Hereford, this shop had the potential to become a supply hub for the area, along with the butcher's shop on the opposite corner of the street. Teresa put all her energies into her new venture and within a short time had some uplifting stories to tell.

"There is one little old lady who shops every day," she told us, "And she sees it as a lifeline to have all the shops she needs within walking distance."

She tells us too of how she sees her role in the community extending beyond merely being the proprietor of a small shop. As an example, she quotes the fact that she is ably assisted in the shop by Michael, whose learning difficulties restrict his job opportunities elsewhere. Teresa took him on as a general help and now she has extended his responsibilities to making deliveries to local customers on the shop bike, as well as doing the banking when Teresa is too busy to leave the shop.

It is Teresa's policy to buy fresh local produce wherever she can, but it is clear that some of her customers, possibly through a simple lack of awareness, still expect to see out-of-season produce all the year round, much as they would in the numerous supermarkets around the city. As a gentle form of education, Teresa has introduced ideas such as a gardening and seed swap club as well as generating an interest in jam and marmalade making, whereby she is calling upon some of the more mature residents to share their knowledge and experience with younger people, thus passing on the skills.

Some residents supply the shop with surplus produce from their own gardens or allotments, and one of them grows plums exclusively for the Fruit Basket. To give this produce pride of place, Teresa puts it on display with the supplier's name on the box. At Christmas time, she makes sure that her Christmas trees are sourced as locally as possible and she has someone making her Christmas wreaths for her too. From May onwards, she also has a local person planting up hanging baskets of flowers for the shop or for private orders.

Inside the shop, the community feel continues with the very homely atmosphere, enhanced by a row of small blackboards on the back wall of the shop, chalked up with a different recipe for each day of the week, supplied by Teresa's customers. They are really useful for generating ideas for using up seasonal gluts, just when many people are beginning to panic about what to do with yet another basket of courgettes. With the emphasis on community and local produce, a delivery system is already operating through Michael. This may well expand into a veg box scheme in the future but, in the meantime, The Fruit Basket has become the local outlet for the Shared Harvest range of hand made breads.

What this small shop requires to ensure its success in the future is the support of the local community Teresa wants to serve. Thus there is a pressing need for the local residents to understand clearly what an asset this little place is and how it actually represents a future way of shopping rather than a relic from the past. It is dispiriting to think that some people will quite happily walk past a shop like this to buy their vegetables from M&S, yet, in our topsy-turvy world, it is only to be expected. M&S has a gigantic marketing budget that can put their name in front of millions of people at the same time. Teresa has no marketing budget at all. Her quiet voice of reason is no match for the voice-overs on the prime-time TV ads run by M&S. Nevertheless, shops like The Fruit Basket are vital to our future security.

None of us has any real idea of how the major challenges that we face as a society, that is to say the problems of Peak Oil and climate change, will encroach on our accepted way of life in the future, but one pronouncement that can be made with some certainty is that change will surely happen. Our modern food supply system depends on a finely honed just-in-time global delivery system that is totally dependent on access to cheap fossil fuel; this applies to 'your M&S' as much as to any other corporate retailer. An increase in price or a reduction in its availability will impinge detrimentally on our food security with potentially disastrous consequences. In 2000, after a relatively brief strike by tanker drivers, our food stocks were so drastically reduced that there was only enough food left to feed the nation for three days, a situation that the New Economics Foundation has described as 'nine meals from anarchy.'

Undoubtedly, there is a pressing need to safeguard our food security. Recognising the value of community-minded people like Teresa, and the worth to the community of shops like The Fruit Basket, is now a matter of priority. However, in order to understand this fully, we firstly have to accept that food at one time formed the hub which turned the wheels of community, that sharing our food with others is a primal act of humanity which binds us to each other, and that there is an urgent need to get back to this concept in the future.

The main hindrance to such understanding is that the connection between us and our food has been broken. No longer aware of the true effort that goes into the production of food, we are unable to see what a precious resource it is. In a world where some children cannot make the link between potatoes and chips, or burgers and bullocks, how many people actually know anything about food at all? Where does it all come from? Leaving out of the argument for the moment that too much of it comes from distant lands, let's look instead at the mechanics of food production. Just for instance, every vegetable has to be planted, tended, thinned out, irrigated, nurtured to maturity, harvested and possibly packed, and then the ground has to be prepared for the next batch. Every pork chop, every rack of lamb, every sirloin steak, were all once part of an animal that has been born and, in the right environment, reared, cared for, fed and kept free of disease and distress until the time comes for us to bring its life to an end, so that we can eat meat. The ruthlessness of intensive farming means that many corners are cut from these processes, yet they still fundamentally remain as acts of growing, rearing and harvesting.

Food is truly precious. It keeps us alive, and nutritious food keeps us out of the doctor's. Cheap food is industrial food, and it damages our health – that's the kind of Government Health Warning we should be given, not the idiotic exhortations to avoid real foods. Without wishing to be dubbed a conspiracy theorist, I feel that the malodorous whiff of suspicion emanates from any collaboration between Government departments and the agri-businesses that lobby them, and I trust no one where the making of money is a prime motivator. The corporate retailers have for many decades sold us the message that food is cheap and then, in an act of jaw-dropping disingenuousness, have compounded this untruth by blaming the consumer for demanding cheap food in the first place.

No one made such demands until the supermarkets invited us to believe that cheap food is some kind of birthright. But cheap food is all about competitive rivalry, with the biggest operators slugging it out to be the cheapest in town, and all of them using devices such as loss leaders or 2-for-1 offers to get customers in through their doors. Cheap food? It is only cheap because the true cost is being borne elsewhere. The cost of loss leader discounts and in-store offers is usually loaded onto the suppliers, as the supermarkets don't like to diminish their profitability. Then there is the food itself, degraded in order to make it less expensive to produce, and therefore more profitable to sell. And finally, we bear the cost ourselves – cheap food compromises our overworked immune systems and leaves us open to the diseases of industrialisation.

We have become myopic in our inability to apply to food the same maxim as we so readily apply elsewhere: you get what you pay for. A realistic approach to food and the policies that keep supermarket prices at rock bottom will stimulate clarity of vision. Once we see that food is indeed a precious gift and not merely a route to profit for the food industry, we can begin once again to build a relationship with what should be our primary source of health, and build it through communal support.

Even in a recession, supermarkets tend to post impressive profit figures. Yet the food processors and industrial agri-businesses that supply this market also make handsome profits. It does not take a mathematical genius to see that, if all these companies are making a profit on rock bottom retail prices, something somewhere has to give, and someone has to be losing out. Well, someone is. It's us. We are the ones at the end of the line. We must learn that the vast 'choice' filling the supermarket shelves is just a delusion, and nothing more than reflections in a hall of mirrors. There might be forty different packets of cereals on show but, inside the box, the stuff is just variations on a theme by Kellogg, all of them processed and all so nutritionally depleted that vitamins have to be added by law.

Once realisation illuminates our thinking, and we understand how precious a resource real food is, the need to source it locally brings with it the kind of cooperation that builds communities. Thus the wheel comes full circle and, in our modern world, we might learn to reclaim something we began to lose our grip on when industrialisation created what is effectively an alien way of life.

"One can say everything best over a meal."
George Eliot [Adam Bede]

The first year of the 21st Century saw my marriage of twenty-five years on the rocks, and I found myself living alone in a two-bedroomed flat. The second bedroom was for my younger son, Ed, who reluctantly found himself having to divide his time between his estranged parents. His older brother, George, had a home of his own, so it didn't affect him in quite the same way, but Ed was only fifteen and still at school. During the time he spent with me in these unfamiliar surroundings, I felt it important to provide him with as stable an atmosphere as possible, and I quite instinctively turned to food as the fundamental catalyst to stability.

From the time we are born with a primary reliance on our mother's milk, the link between food and human bonding is undeniable, and in my flat Ed and I shared that bond by sharing food. Although it was only the two of us, without thinking about it I went through the ritual of laying up the table for breakfast, so that we could have that time together in the morning before he went to school. Without the distraction of radio or Breakfast Television, we were simply able to be ourselves, sitting at our little kitchen table with just two places laid. Breakfast might have been not much more than a bowl of cereal, some toast and a hot drink, but it was a meal that we were eating together, and the unspoken and unwritten significance of this communal act was profound.

The philosophy of Winnie-the-Pooh

"When you wake up in the morning, Pooh" said Piglet at last, "what's the first thing you say to yourself?"
"What's for breakfast?" said Pooh. "What do you say, Piglet?"
"I say, I wonder what's going to happen exciting to-day?" said Piglet.
Pooh nodded thoughtfully.
"It's the same thing," he said.

On his return from school, I would cook a meal for Ed and we would go through the minimal table-laying ceremony again, with some place mats, knives and forks and perhaps a glass for a drink. Once again, we were able to enjoy the experience of eating together before Ed went out to go skateboarding or playing basketball with his mates. Our evening meal may have been nothing more than a one pot wonder, or even something like spaghetti with a Bolognese sauce, but I always made it fresh and, if Ed was home in time from school, he would be with me in the kitchen as I was preparing it. The essential importance of sharing the experience of food, whether that involves growing, cooking, eating or all three, simply cannot be overestimated.

During that brief time when Ed had to divide his life between two homes, it was the communion of sharing food that enabled him to relax in the unfamiliar surroundings of the flat his Dad now occupied. Eating communally, even if there are only two people involved, connects us at an emotional level. At those times when Ed was with his mother, and I was eating alone, I would still go through the motions of laying a place at table for myself, preparing something to eat and then sitting down and eating. By doing that, I was at least preserving the vestiges of communion, even if it was communing only with my food.

What was happening in my flat was perfectly understandable. Food brings people together, and eating communally creates a bond at a profound spiritual level. Religion has been quick to understand this and many religious orders throughout the world combine food and ritual as a central theme. Though we are presently lost in what amounts to a vast and featureless food desert, if we are to find our way back to the land of plenty we must understand the role food plays in community. Food makes community, but it must be real food as defined in the preceding chapters. It is only real food that has the power to re-create our lost communities, because it is real food that involves us in growing, cooking and eating, all of which by definition become communal acts carried out at a local level.

Beef in Stout

There are so many recipes for 'big stews' to be found in books such as Elizabeth Luard's The Rich Tradition of European Peasant Cookery, but their essential purpose is the same in every case – to provide a nourishing meal that can be enjoyed by a number of people eating together and sharing the same pot. There is something particularly comforting about having a big pot of something aromatic as the centrepiece of a family meal.

Taking a very basic idea that probably began in Belgium, the kingdom of beers, we do our own version of Boeuf à la Flamande, using Organic Oatmeal Stout from one of our excellent local breweries, the Spinning Dog brewery in Hereford.

This is a good winter recipe, so I have used pickling onions, because they look nice in the stew. If you don't have pickling onions, any onions will do – it's the flavour that's important more than the look. If they are large, simply quarter them, or even slice them thickly.

For up to 6 people, you will need:
2lbs shin of beef, diced
olive oil
20 pickling onions, peeled
4 fat cloves of garlic, sliced
1tbs (heaped) unbleached flour
3 bay leaves
6 sprigs of thyme
2 x 500ml bottles of beer
sea salt and black pepper

Heat a few tablespoons of olive oil in a good frying pan. Brown the chunks of beef well on all sides and, using a slotted spoon, transfer to a casserole pot. Fry the onions and garlic in the same oil for a few minutes before adding them to the meat in the pot. Stir the flour into the oil and juices left in the pan and stir fry for a minute or two until the flour begins to brown and give off a lovely aroma. Add the beer and bring to the boil, stirring to avoid lumps while the sauce thickens. Season with sea salt and black pepper, then pour the sauce into the casserole with the bay leaves and thyme. Bake at 180°C for about 2½ hours. For the ultimate treat, serve this with mashed potatoes* and any vegetables that might be around at the time.

* I'm not going to give you a recipe for mashed potatoes, but I'll give you a hint about how to make them really tasty – mash in at least 2oz of butter per pound of potatoes! Season with salt, pepper and freshly grated nutmeg, and fluff it up with an electric whisk just before serving.

Industrial food is dead food that requires no spiritual commitment from us in its consumption. It has been an interesting experiment for some, but it is of no further use to us and we must take steps to eliminate it from our lives. We must bring real food back to life and revive its soul for, by doing so, we revive our own souls too. What industrialisation has done is to remove our reverence for food and condemn the food itself to the life of a mere commodity. Thus have we abused the gift of nourishment, and by eating such abused foods we simply abuse ourselves. Our souls suffer as we replace quality with quantity and replace communal meals with eating on our own whilst walking down the street.

Real food inspires reverence, breeds conviviality and gives us pleasure. Its soul thrives on social ritual, good manners and a sense of style, all manifestations of eating communally. This opens the door to true social values. It is the difference between simply surviving and really living, between eating to live and living to eat, between going through the motions of keeping ourselves fed and living in a world of beauty, elegance and social stability. The ritual, manners and style around food need not be complex. Ed and I didn't complicate our simple breakfast ritual, but we wouldn't let a morning go without it. Such simple and graceful acts of formality elevate the experience of eating. So often these days, the experience is debased, now that we live in a world where manners and style are seen as quaint old-fashioned ideas. Eating without ceremony is the general approach today, but this saddens the soul and we unwittingly and simultaneously depress all aspects of our lives to the lowest common denominator. Thus, in another manifestation of the same malady, if people no longer dress up to go out, it is not because it is particularly unfashionable to do so. More often than not, it is because they just can't be bothered.

Losing the connectedness with our food has smothered our desire to eat communally, so community spirit withers, hearts harden and we become more insular. Putting to flight the soul of food has allowed the dark side of industrialisation to dominate. Though this has grown into a global problem, the solution is personal. Each one of us can help to bring about the revival and put the soul back into food. Let's take more time to get together to grow more of our own, in our gardens, on our smallholdings and farms, even on our balconies and windowsills. That way, we will regain respect for what we eat. Let's teach each other to cook. Cooking with and for others is in itself an act of communal celebration. Preparing food to eat should inspire joy. It should not be seen as a chore. The act of preparing and cooking food helps to refine us, slow us down, give us time to reflect and ponder. Quite simply, it is good for the soul, and it shows us how to live: creatively, lovingly, patiently and observantly. To go through this process of re-acquainting ourselves with real food, to share the elements of growing, cooking and eating together will open our minds to how food creates community and how community creates the basis on which our future depends.

Chapter Ten

Eat . . . like there's no tomorrow

For many years, I maintained that the four cornerstones of life are music, food, sex and sleep, preferably in that order. Now, as I begin to bask in the sunshine of understanding, I have come to modify my outlook. It appears to me, with all due homage to Abraham Maslow and his Hierarchy of Needs, that life's four cornerstones are in fact music, touch (intimacy), sleep and play, in no particular order, and that these must be built on a foundation of food for the edifice to stand steady.

Food (and, as ever, I mean real food) is the firmest base on which we can construct a social community of true human values. It is a great socialiser. It civilises us, and it suppresses our innate disposition to violence. That so many religious orders include food as a central idea is quite understandable, and the symbolism of 'breaking bread' is profound. It is significant that those who respond positively to my calls for change in *The Food Maze* begin by making their own bread for the family. There is a fascination in being involved in the alchemy which begins with the simple act of combining flour and water and letting it stand for a while in a warm place. Of course we can add salt and other ingredients for flavour, and we can speed up the procedure by adding yeast, but making bread is still a fundamental symbol of creating from simple ingredients a food which is best when shared. As such, it is an icon of the idea of community.

Recently, Wigmores Bakery in Monmouth, one of the last traditional bakeries in Wales, came up for sale. It was bought, with enough deliberation to be just short of impulsive, by Louise Eklof for her husband, Richard, recent escapee from the high-pressure, cut-throat and demanding world of financial software. Having had enough of such an existence, Richard, Louise and their family moved from Reigate to Monmouth with a view to making some lifestyle changes. After a short time trying to keep his previous business contacts going by commuting to London from Monmouth, Richard decided that this idea had no long-term future, and Louise wanted back the person he was before he became obsessed by the pursuit of wealth. They both needed something at a local level that would allow them to live life at a different pace. Some might say that taking on an ailing traditional bakery and completely revitalising it is no way to achieve that pace, but they would be wrong. Though there is undoubtedly a huge effort required in running this kind of small operation, there are rewards that more than compensate.

Not least of these is the community aspect of the business. Richard is finding there is something very fulfilling about looking after people's needs at a human level. He has his pet customers, like his 'little old ladies' who want to buy only half a loaf at a time, and he cares about making bread that stands out against the debased and degraded products more generally available. Learning as he goes from skilled bakers now employed at Wigmores, Richard is fast becoming a master baker himself. Active in seeking outlets for his traditional bread amongst the local schools, independent shops and markets, he is helping to spread the word that his traditional bread is tastier and healthier than the industrial alternative more usually bought by such establishments. His business is growing and he has employed more staff. It is less than two years since he took on the bakery, but his staff has increased from the five he inherited to eighteen today.

At one point, Richard was offered the opportunity to make bread for a small chain of shops with 500 outlets, but this is of no interest to him as he understands that he would have to compromise the product in order to supply on this scale. Keeping the quality of his bread consistently high is one of his priorities, and he will not degrade the product simply to increase his turnover. This doesn't mean that he has no plans for expansion, however; he has already created another outlet in Abergavenny, taking on another business that needed a shot of enthusiasm to revitalise it. No doubt he may find the opportunity to expand again but, from talking to him, I would say that he will do this only if he can continue to make high quality traditional bakery goods that represent value for money to local customers. Meanwhile, he is working on increasing the range of cakes and patisseries available at his shop, as well as moving into the lunchtime sandwich and take-away market, but the emphasis remains firmly on supplying a local customer base with efficacious products.

Richard is a local baker serving a local community, and he is committed to raising awareness of the community benefits of dealing with a local firm. To be able to go into Wigmores, where the bread is being baked by the people on the premises is an asset not recognised by most. The value of it, in social and human terms, cannot be over-emphasised, primarily because a meaningful dialogue can take place directly between producer and customer. If, for instance, the customer wants a particular kind of loaf or a cake for a family party, the request can be made, and Richard is there to respond to his customers by having that conversation with them as people from the same community.

In building a community structure which will be resilient to the violent winds of change that might ravage our currently precarious food system, we must clearly understand our own role in its construction. Enterprises such as Wigmores, The Fruit Basket, Carey Organic, Cameron & Swan, Emma's Pigs and all the other similar ventures that are springing up around the country cannot survive without our support. The brave people who set up these ventures have done all the hard work for us – all we have to do is to buy from them. How hard can that be? Especially when what is on offer is vastly superior to the degraded industrial products they rival, and when they are able to engage us directly in conversation to discuss our needs. There is really no contest, and no reason that I can think of to continue to buy industrial food.

"White flour, with the live germ taken out of it after being squashed between steel rollers, is as dead and as 'keepable' as Portland cement powder – and about as fit for food."
Cmdr Geoffrey Bowles RN : November 1942

The comment above, written nearly seventy years ago by Commander Geoffrey Bowles, the original Mr Angry and uncle to the famous Mitford sisters, speaks volumes about industrial food, focusing as it does on the lifeless white powder sold to us as wholesome flour. The iconic status of real bread as the central theme of shared food has been completely undermined by the arrival of bleached white flour. It has given rise to that symbol of the new industrial age, the standard sliced factory loaf, now an icon in its own right. So enduring is its image that the expression, 'the best thing since sliced bread,' has not only entered the language but has already become so overused as to warrant cliché status.

Industrial bread is not real bread at all. Real bread takes time to develop, part of a simple process that goes back centuries. In a factory, time is money, so time must be taken out of the equation. Most factory bread today is made by the Chorleywood Bread Process, which speeds everything up. Additives must be added to bolster the dough and prevent it from collapsing, as this kind of loaf surely would if it was simply a mixture of lifeless flour, water, yeast and salt. Modern day factory bread hasn't the strength to support its own weight once air bubbles get into it, so the Chorleywood process introduces a synthetic support system that has been devised to hold it up just long enough to get it baked. Into the mixture also go additives to make it taste of something other than cotton wool, mould inhibitors to give it shelf life and perhaps a preservative or two. Regarding its status as a food, it cannot be denied that a factory loaf contains protein, carbohydrate, fat and fibre, the proportions of which are listed in the ludicrously irrelevant 'nutritional information' emblazoned on every pack. As for real nutrition – forget it. You would probably be better off going hungry.

"How can a nation be great if its bread tastes like Kleenex?"
Julia Child [1912 – 2004]

From the notion of the 'breaking of bread' as a symbol of fraternity, humanity and spirituality, we have strayed into a world of distorted metaphors, a grotesque mockery of the real thing, and the white sliced loaf epitomises what has gone wrong, not just with our food, but possibly with life itself. Bread, that icon of community and sharing, that physical manifestation of the soul of society, has been usurped by this sly fraud, and we now live in a world where veracity is obscured by deception. We are no more than dazed revellers at a fun fair, wandering aimlessly through a hall of mirrors, no longer able to distinguish which is the true reflection of real life. In our culinary theme park, we have embraced the fast food dream of permanent global summertime and the implied luxury of having everything all the time. Like so many honeybees flitting from flower to flower in a colourful herbaceous border, we wallow in what looks like a limitless array of foods, yet the boundaries of choice are actually contained within a narrow band of duplications and variations on a theme provided for us by a cloned regiment of food factories. And the real bees are dying in their millions, overworked by us in our desire for honey, to the extent that their battered immune systems, like our own, are leaving them vulnerable. Ravaged by pesticides and compromised to such an extent that they can no longer protect themselves from viral attack, these essential little ecological lynchpins are disappearing. Like canaries in a mineshaft, bees are our early warning system that we could be next if we don't fix our food.

Like any theme park, what we see is artificial, one-dimensional and without depth. Eating and drinking on the hoof shows a breakdown of our relationship with food, as we simply fuel our bodies without feeding our souls. The breakdown of our bodies in succumbing to the diseases of industrialisation leads us further into the wilderness, as we

151

ask all the wrong questions about what is amiss, and so are met with all the wrong answers. In a seemingly self-harming bid to contradict Darwin's theory, we have tipped the scales of our own evolution. It appears that each succeeding generation, in the industrialised world at least, is getting weaker rather than stronger then the previous one. Government and the medical profession would vehemently disagree with such a claim, yet the statistics reveal a rising tide of food-related diseases and disorders afflicting younger and younger people.

No longer able to understand why the problems have occurred, we become paranoid. A new kind of Puritanism stalks society, breeding food phobias, distrust, wariness and guilt about our food, as we draw up a list of foods we deny ourselves, only for our resolve to crumble as we fall into the temptation to eat them. The diet industry has grown fat on these insecurities, whilst we have not grown thin, thus failing to fulfil that ideal imposed upon us by an image-conscious, celebrity-obsessed world of spin and deceit. We must feel for those who fall prey to this kind of hype and slide into the murky depths of anorexia and bulimia.

It is imperative that we help them and help ourselves by recognising the advertising industry's wickedness for what it is and reclaiming our common sense. We have to teach ourselves to eat once again, but moderately and with pleasure. Eating and pleasure are natural partners, and the enjoyment comes from choosing our foods carefully. There is no joy in eating ascetically, hooked into some spurious diet regime that denies us the foods we want. But beware those wants, for they may be cravings in disguise, and thus may indicate an addiction to the main constituents of processed foods – sugar, salt and artificial flavourings. Eat real food and those wants and cravings will disappear.

In re-skilling ourselves in the art of eating, it is crucial that we recognise the terminally damaging effect of industrialisation on our food. It has killed our fertile soils, poisoned our aquifers, tainted our seas and decimated the planet's ecology. Make no mistake; our soils are barren, our crops and animals are sick and so are we. Gaia herself is ailing, but she will survive by doing what she needs to do to shake off that parasitic, destructive species, *homo sapiens*. If we are to live on this planet, we must earn the right to do so, and that means finding our place within the finely balanced ecosystem that is Mother Earth. Beware those technologists who claim to have found solutions to saving the planet, for their main preoccupation is, more prosaically, *saving humanity from having to change the way it behaves*. It can't be done – we can't 'save the planet' without radically changing the way we do things. We have already gone too far down the wrong route and have trapped ourselves in a cul-de-sac. The time has come to find our way out of this dead end by conducting a major overhaul of our world view, and understanding our place in the overall concept of Gaia. I believe that, by changing the way we eat, we will put ourselves a long way down the route to recovery.

Start here . . . your own home made burger baps

Nothing beats the smell and flavour of home baked bread and, in these days of bread makers, baking bread rolls or even speciality breads couldn't be easier. However, don't be put off by the thought of doing the whole thing by hand. It is really so satisfying to make bread from scratch, taking the simple ingredients of flour, water, yeast, salt and butter and, with a modicum of effort, patience and time, to produce something as tasty and comforting as bread.

Forget the Big Mac, get the kids into the kitchen and try your hand at making your own beefburgers and baps. Feel the satisfaction of knowing exactly what has gone into them. If you are lucky enough to have a local whole food shop that sells fresh yeast then use that in preference to the dried or fast action variety. You will need 2 baking trays greased with butter or lined with baking parchment and the oven set to 220°C.

This recipe has been adapted from Bread Matters by Andrew Whitley – my bread bible and a must for anyone who really wants to get into bread making.

For 12 white baps you will need:
600g strong organic stoneground unbleached white flour
10g fresh yeast or 5g traditional 'active dried' or 3g 'fast-action' yeast
375ml water
5g sea salt
30g softened butter (to enhance dough volume)

In a large bowl, dissolve the yeast in water. This helps to ensure even distribution in the dough. Then gradually combine all the other ingredients and when everything has been incorporated into a single lump, remove to a lightly floured surface and begin to knead. It doesn't matter how this is done so long as the dough is subjected to vigorous handling for at least 10 minutes and until the dough is soft, pliable and has a silky finish. Place the dough in the bowl, cover and leave to rise for 1-2 hours in a warmish place but not on top of a boiler or radiator! Don't worry if you only have a cool place, it just means that this first prove will take longer.

When you are happy that the dough has appreciably expanded, place it on the work surface and without de-gassing it too much, divide it into about 12 equal pieces and mould each one into a flattish round. Dip each one into a bowl of flour and ensure the whole roll is lightly covered. Place the baps about 2 cm apart on a greased baking tray. Cover the whole tray with a loose polythene bag, large enough for the expanding rolls to have enough space to rise without touching the bag. When the baps have risen and taken up their space, remove the bag and bake in the oven for about 15 minutes. They will probably be touching each other so it will be easy to check if they are done by gently tearing one away from the rest. If the interior looks underdone, give them a couple more minutes. Remove the tray from the oven, place the baps on a wire rack to cool.

As the 21st Century rolls out, the question we are beginning to hear more and more is: what kind of a world have we created? Our legacy from two hundred years of industrialisation (a period characterised by imperial dominance, greed, international conflict and the creation of consumerism and mass poverty) is a damaged and exploited world now facing unpredictable climate change and the decline of oil, a substance in fixed supply with which we have been profligate to the point of lunacy. It is likely that we have already passed the point of no return as regards repairing our damaged climate. It is almost certain that we have already reached what is referred to as 'peak oil', that point beyond which the amount we are able to extract from the earth decreases year by year, an alarming situation exacerbated by increasing demand. Some of our brightest thinkers are so worried by the implications of these two challenges that they are suggesting this might be the last century for our species. I would argue that it will quite likely be the last century of life as we have known it, but that our species is resilient, and will probably survive, albeit in very much smaller numbers. However, I also believe that the real elephant in the room, the degradation of our food, is the greatest challenge we face, and it would do no harm to address this issue.

There are many noteworthy organisations currently involved in bringing to our attention the implications of climate change and peak oil, yet far too little is being said about how our globalised factory food system underpins and contributes to them. Helping to fix our food is the one thing each one of us can do on an immediate daily basis to begin to tackle those other major challenges. Surely we need no further incentive to do this than the understanding that industrial food damages us and our world. This poor quality food has made us prone to diseases such as diabetes, atherosclerosis, various heart conditions and cancers. We are kept alive by increasingly sophisticated medical techniques and a staggeringly high ingestion of pharmaceutical products, supplied to us by yet another global industry that relies heavily on the availability of cheap oil, but that's not the point. The issue is quite clear. We have been duped. The Emperor of New Foods is not dressed in the finery we are being asked to believe in, but is in fact naked. The traditional foods that have sustained us for millennia have been demonised over the last 50 years, and we have been told to avoid many of them at all costs. We have been told that if we don't we risk blocked arteries, heart attacks and premature death. But this is all a complete and blatant lie, and the opposite is in fact true – real foods, including animal fats and dairy products from grass-fed animals, sustain us, whilst synthesised foods make us ill.

Industrial food is made by industry, and industry is motivated not by the health of its customers but by profit. Industry has become so powerful that it threatens not only our health but also the health of our whole planet. Agri-business covers millions of acres of would-be farmland right across the world with endless monocultures of cash crops that feed the processing industry, not people. This is not true farming; it is simply using agricultural land to run a business, and businesses demand a specific kind of efficiency. For the sake of conforming to the requirements of global agri-business, crop varieties around the world have been whittled down to a handful of specified hybrids, resulting in a huge loss of biodiversity. The production of our own food is now effectively out of our control. If we allow this situation to continue without intervention, we lose control over what happens to us and the planet in the future. Without a doubt, abdication of responsibility has left us vulnerable to the sharp practices of a profit-motivated food industry. Things look bad, but not half as bad as they will look in the future if something is not done to reverse humanity's slide into oblivion.

You may be forgiven for thinking that I am in danger of losing it, tripping into hysteria or exaggerating for effect. Yet, consider this. Our food supply is now firmly in the hands of what has been described as a corporatocracy. Global behemoths like Monsanto, Cargill, Archer Daniels Midland (ADM), Smithfield Foods and Dean Foods control worldwide agriculture, farming, processing and distribution. At the retail end, we have trans-national corporations like Wal-Mart, Tesco, Carrefour and a dozen others who vie with each other for control of retail food distribution.

In the same way that an ant may not notice the elephant standing behind him, we cannot see a company like Cargill, to take one very big example. Hiding behind a collection of 'brand names' acquired during the course of its growth (Cargill, just for instance, owns Sun Valley, the industrial chicken business often cited as one of

'Herefordshire's success stories'), the global corporation often does not reveal itself in its true form. It morphs and shape-shifts through a number of different identities until finally, perhaps in a show of confidence brought on by the impregnability of sheer size, it finally unveils its true self. I speak from personal observation, having seen the name 'Sun Valley' for years displayed as a sponsor on the hoardings around the Hereford United football ground, and then seeing that name changed recently to 'Cargill,' as it has been outside the Sun Valley factory gates.

I wonder how many people have noticed this change or made the link between the two names. Obviously many people in Hereford work for Cargill, but what about those to whom the name means nothing? I even wonder how much Cargill's Herefordshire employees actually know about the company. Often quoted as the world's largest private company, it is also one of its most secretive. As a private company in the USA, it is under no obligation to publish detailed accounts. Brewster Kneen, author of *Invisible Giant,* describes Cargill as 'the undisputed ruler in the global grain trade' with tentacles that extend into 'every aspect of the global food system.' Cargill itself is a little more grandiose in its own self-assessment of its global position. In the company brochures, according to Felicity Lawrence in *Eat Your Heart Out*, it states, 'We buy, trade, transport, blend, mill, crush, process, refine, season, distribute around the clock, around the globe', and, 'We are the flour in your bread, the wheat in your noodles, the salt on your fries. We are the corn in your tortillas, the chocolate in your dessert, the sweetener in your soft drink. We are the oil in your salad dressing, and the beef, pork or chicken you eat for dinner. We are the cotton in your clothing, the backing on your carpet, and the fertiliser in your field.' The list could go on, with Cargill involved in everything from animal feedstuffs to hedge funds and derivatives trading.

Allowing the responsibility for our food to be under the control of a profit-driven oligopoly leaves us and our environment vulnerable in many ways, but none more serious than the breathtakingly rapid loss of biodiversity it precipitates. It is worth just looking at this a little more closely.

Nature is remarkably clever. By 'nature' I am referring to everything that might be encompassed by the term 'life on Earth'. The evolution of species, through the gradual development of minutely different characteristics suited to particular environments, ensures that any given species has a greater chance of survival. Thus, for instance, many of the wild plants of England also appear in other locations in Northern Europe, but as distinctly different variations on a theme. This principle is fundamental, and has been used by gardeners, growers and animal breeders quite successfully for millennia to produce regional and local varieties that make the best of local conditions. Every gardener effectively became a plant breeder, by doing nothing more complicated than saving the seeds of plants that did best in their own locality. So each gardener was nurturing and maintaining a slightly different strain of any given vegetable, which in turn led to a huge living genebank that became a resilient safeguard against disease, pest attack or changes in climate patterns. Such a model of genepool growth has continued for as long as Man has been farming, a period in excess of 10,000 years. The seeds from our plants over this vast period of time were real or, to put it another way, as nature intended. They were simply collected from what is known as 'open-pollination' and planted in the following year. This is as close to nature as we can get within the formal structure of horticulture or farming.

Now all this has been recklessly squandered for the sake of short-term profits. Over the last half a century, during the rising tide of agri-business, the skills of the old gardeners and plantsmen have floundered. Almost all of our local varieties and individual strains have been lost, replaced by what the seed companies call F1 hybrids, a commercial seed enterprise's ticket to profit. Saving and nurturing seed by traditional means takes care and patience, whereas the production of F1 hybrids requires far less manpower and time, so that's a clear cost-saving for a profit-motivated company. Parent stocks for F1 hybrids are generally heavily inbred, so the seeds from these hybrids will either be sterile or unpredictable. Only the seed company knows anything about the parent stock for any given variety. If you want to grow a particular vegetable again next year, it is pointless to save the seed from an F1 hybrid, because of the unpredictable results, so you have to buy direct from the seed company each year. Great for the company's profits, but not for your pocket.

Losing our choice of viable real seeds is potentially disastrous, as it removes the safeguards that diversity ensures. Worse than that, though, seeds today are simply bred for large industrial farms that represent big profits. Small time gardeners merely get drip-fed a few of these through garden centres and the like. The industrial farms are locked into the supermarket system, so they are also subject to the whims of supermarket buyers. If the supermarkets want straighter leeks or more pointy carrots, their suppliers conform readily to these demands. Thus even the choice of F1 hybrids is gradually being whittled down as the supermarkets continue to rationalise the vegetable 'products' on offer. At the commodity end of agriculture, where the gigantic grain traders like Cargill or ADM demand uniformity to supply avaricious processors such as Nestlé, Kraft Foods, Unilever and Premier Foods, the loss of biodiversity has been spectacular. From the thousands of species of maize, wheat and rice that once existed on the Earth, we are down to just a tiny handful of hybrid varieties that suit the processes the food industry subjects them to. An insistence on uniformity from fast food chains like McDonald's and processors like McCain has meant that, from a diverse range that once encompassed hundreds of local varieties, there are now no more than three potato varieties that are regularly grown by big commercial growers in the USA. It is much the same story in the UK. Worldwide, 75% of the food we eat is produced from only 12 plant types and five animal species. The future looks bleak. At the very least, such loss of biodiversity leaves crops vulnerable to attack from virus, fungus or insect.

Another gem from the wartime Mr Angry . . .

"Combines and Big Business intend, by war-time 'planning' methods, to accustom the people of England to murdered food. No food is to be left with the life that heaven and earth and sunlight gave it. All is to be de-vitalised, de-natured, de-hydrated, de-everythinged and generally bedevilled with chemicals and heat and processes and tins, and be spoilt in every kind of way in order to sell and to 'keep.' The mass of our people is never to eat fresh food. Practically no food is as good as it used to be."

Cmdr Geoffrey Bowles RN : November 1942

How much has been written by others, and how much more could I write now, about the deathly kiss of industrialisation on our health? Another book could easily come out of it. It is not my wish, however, to labour the point. We all know, deep in our souls, that the creation of processed foods and the mantra that 'farming is a business like any other' has been one of the greatest disasters of the 20th Century. Yet the corporations that have a grip on our food supply and are choking the very life out of us and our planet can see little more than their bottom line, and will continue unchecked to do whatever is necessary to maintain their profitability. Little more can be gained here from detailing their behaviour, but allow me to quote one more example of what we are up against.

Through the writings of many eminent authors, it has become clear that most processed foods are so bland, so offensively uninteresting and so lacking in taste that the manufacturers have, over the years, been adding increasing amounts of sugar, salt and additives such as monosodium glutamate in order to fool us into thinking that we are consuming something tasty. Sugar, salt and the other additives have now become a matter of concern in government and medical circles. The food industry is under pressure to reduce these ingredients, and thus is faced with the dilemma of how to do that without reducing their processed foods to a level of blandness that would detrimentally affect sales. Galloping to their rescue is a company called Senomyx, taking food technology to new frontiers.

Senomyx is a relatively new biotechnology company based in San Diego, and their claim to fame is that they have developed a range of chemicals for the food industry that trick the taste buds into sensing flavours, such as salty or sweet, when they are not really there. By using information from the human genome, Senomyx has identified hundreds of taste receptors in the mouth and worked out how to turn these on and off. The company collaborates with the world's largest food processors, including Kraft Foods, Cadbury Schweppes, the Campbell Soup Company, Coca Cola and Nestlé. Their patented discoveries mean that these global food giants can now legitimately claim that their products contain less sugar and salt, because the Senomyx additives have altered the way in which food is tasted, in such a way that we do not notice that the salt or sugar content has gone down. How far will technology go in tampering with our foods in order to support the profitability of these companies at the expense of our wellbeing? The answer is: as far as they have to. Which of course prompts the next question: what better reason do we have to change the way we eat?

We are told by the proponents of our global food industry that, as a result of their tireless and ceaseless efforts, we have come out of the age of subsistence farming to enjoy the fruits of the Earth in an abundance undreamed of by our forefathers. They have made it so easy for us. All we need to do is to pop into the supermarket and choose from an overflowing cornucopia that gives us the choice of everything from everywhere anytime. What more could we want?

Well, firstly we want some nutrition, and then we want a system of food production that works constructively with nature, not destructively. We want the kind of farming that does not poison the land, the waterways, the underground aquifers and the seas. We want an agricultural approach that understands the holistic nature of our tiny planet and recognises that we humans are no more than one part of the very big jigsaw of life on that planet. We want real food – the kind of food that has sustained us through the centuries and for which our digestive systems have evolved to cope. We want food that will make us grow strong and healthy, not food that fills us with empty calories, toxic additives and unnatural laboratory concoctions. We want to get well again and rebuild our immune systems to be our protection in times of bodily stress. We want to rid ourselves of the diseases of industrialisation. We want equality, compassion and mutual understanding to help those in need to be better fed, instead of suffering the embarrassment of being a part of a morbidly obese culture living in indifferent ignorance of the fact that the other half of the world is dying. That's not too much to ask, is it?

Nourishment is the foundation on which all life is built, whether we are talking about bodily or spiritual life, but somewhere along the line of our social development this principle has been lost. In my writing, I talk about my memories of food, from gathering apples in Grandpa's orchard, or helping my Mum in the kitchen, to cooking a Christmas Eve supper for family and friends, but I feel very much that I am talking a foreign language understood by too few people these days.

Food connects us, but we have lost the connection because we have lost our food. Through industrialisation and its inherent destruction of vitality the true essence of nourishment has died. In its place we have what Michael Pollan has called a range of 'edible food-like substances.' Modern food has virtually no nutrients to sustain the body, thus the modern way of eating has no nutrients for the soul. We have seen in the preceding chapters something of what has gone wrong with our food, and I hope we have seen some indication of what we can do to rectify the situation. There is an urgent need to change our ways, for our destruction is assured if we continue on our present course. All our ills, and the ills of the world, have come about as a result of Man pitting himself against Nature. It is a fight which has no relevance in the natural order of things and is therefore a fight that will have to end. The instigator, Man, will be vanquished, for his actions are contrary to the harmony that keeps our planet in perpetual balance.

One thing is obvious. The 'powers-that-be' will do nothing to change the status quo. Change must come from each one of us. If enough of us simply make the decision that we will no longer buy into the industrial food system, thereby showing unequivocally that it is not what we want, we set ourselves apart from it, and beyond its influence. We in turn create new influence by the power of democracy (something we do not have at present) and by creating demand for real food. We can change the way things are done by changing the way we ourselves do things. It is not up to anyone else. The solution is in our own hands, and it involves surprisingly little effort. We do not have to subscribe to any organisation, we do not have to go to any meetings or wave any banners. We just have to look at the natural world beyond all the trappings of humankind and say, "This is my home and I want to look after it." The quickest and most effective way to begin to do this is to reclaim our right to real nutritious food. By definition, this opens the way to a radical rethink of how that food is produced, and we will find ourselves involved, because growing, cooking and eating the food that sustains us puts us back in tune with nature and makes us grateful for her bounty.

Those of us who make the decision to change will not be alone. The pendulum of change has already begun to swing in a new direction. There are examples all over the country (one might say, all over the world) of new initiatives, such as Community Supported Agriculture schemes, garden share schemes, a new interest in allotments and even spontaneous outbreaks of 'guerrilla gardening,' where people take it upon themselves to commandeer wasteland, unused parkland or even roadside verges in order to grow fruit and vegetables for community use. All such ideas are laudable and an essential part of the process of change. But, for those of us who, for whatever reason, cannot become involved in such a scheme, an individual contribution is just as valid. A change of attitude, whether private or communal, is the essential element of what is required, and each facet of this positive change is as important as any other.

So, let's all grow more, not because growing vegetables has become a trendy thing to do, but because we want to be involved with the food we eat. Let's learn to cook, not because we want to emulate some celebrity TV chef, but because we want to be involved in the preparation of our own food. And let's learn how to eat again, because eating is a fundamental human activity that brings us pleasure, binds us together at a spiritual level and nourishes body and soul. Each change that any one of us makes contributes to the bigger change that is already happening. Be part of that change and take those first steps towards reclaiming what has been quietly taken from us. We will just as quietly take it back.

We owe it to ourselves, but more importantly to those who will inherit this Earth, our children and our children's children, for whose future world we are the current custodians. Will we be able to face them, knowing what we now know, without doing all we can to repair the damage? The onus is without question on us to embark on this journey to re-establish our connection with nature, restore biodiversity and fix our food. It is not difficult for each of us to add our own personal contribution to the solution and thus to know that we are actually doing something that will contribute to the health of the planet, that will protect us from ill health and will help us enjoy the rich bounty nature has to offer without squandering it. There is not much time left, and we must learn once more to nurture the source of our bounty, otherwise it will most certainly slip though our fingers, and there will be no tomorrow.

"The Earth does not belong to Man; Man belongs to the Earth. This we know. Whatever befalls the earth befalls the sons of the earth. Man did not weave the web of life; he is merely a strand in it. Whatever he does to the web, he does to himself."

Chief Seattle (attributed)

Like Robin Hood, Chief Seattle's legacy has become swathed in myth and legend, yet whatever is the source of the words above, they are irrefutably true.

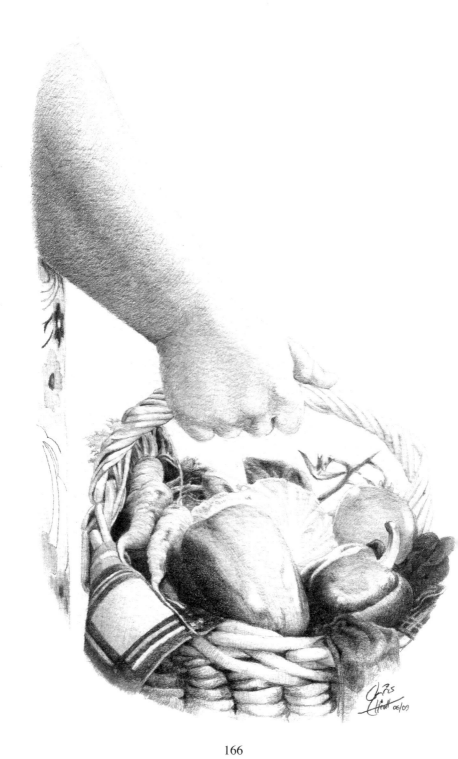

166

Epilogue

In a typically self-effacing comment, that great scientist, Sir Isaac Newton, once modestly qualified his immense achievements by saying, "If I have seen further, it is only by standing on the shoulders of giants." The giants to whom he referred were some of the most illustrious polymaths and philosophical thinkers of the so-called Scientific Revolution – Descartes, Copernicus, Galileo and Kepler. Newton lived at a time when science was still an observational and experimental discipline based on instinct and experience. Our natural inquisitiveness as a species creates the means by which such gifted pioneers flourished in their desire to find out how the world works.

Unfortunately, things have changed. Slowly, stealthily and surreptitiously, science has been commandeered by self-serving individuals and companies for their own ends. Increasingly over the last hundred years or so, this has led to the situation prevalent today, where much scientific research is so corrupted as to be unworthy of the name. Funded by global corporations, particularly in the food and pharmaceutical industries, this kind of research does not ask the simple questions, "Why?" or "How?" Researchers today are effectively told the result that is required, and their task is to find a method that will produce the right answer, enabling corporations to rely heavily on virtually meaningless phrases such as 'scientifically proven.' It gives them the only authority they need to sell us inferior industrial foodstuffs.

So where are the giants upon whose shoulders a modern day Newton might stand? Surprisingly, they are still there, and always have been. If we listen hard enough, their voices can be heard from time to time but, since the Industrial Revolution got up a head of steam, they have been shouted down by the clamour of new opportunists with no other thought but to make their fortunes. More recently, during the rise of the corporations, those quiet voices of reason have been drowned in the uproar of corporate lobbying, demanding protection, favourable legislation and funding from compliant governments across the industrial world.

Nonetheless, those voices persisted, as they earnestly tried to tell us that we were heading for self-destruction. As long ago as 1824, the greenhouse effect was predicted by a Frenchman, Jean Baptise Fourier, and by 1896, the Swedish chemist, Svante Arrhenius, concluded that industrial carbon dioxide emissions were enhancing the greenhouse effect and would lead to climate change. During the early part of the 20th Century, others foretold the consequences of our folly in exploiting our fertile lands, polluting them with chemicals and producing industrial food.

In 1936 in this country, Sir Robert McCarrison spelled out in explicit terms how poor nutrition from degraded foodstuffs was damaging us. His findings were echoed in 1939 by that great American researcher, Weston A. Price, whose studies of indigenous communities across the world confirmed that good nutrition breeds strong healthy people. Later, in 1943, Lady Eve Balfour, a co-founder of The Soil Association, proved unequivocally that polluting our soils with chemical inputs had a disastrous effect upon those soils, upon the plants grown in those soils, the animals that fed on the plants and the humans who feed on the animals. Twenty years after this, Rachel Carson, an American biologist, published her groundbreaking and quite terrifying denunciation of chemical farming, *Silent Spring*, pointing out in the starkest of terms how those chemicals were precipitating what was effectively mass slaughter of our wildlife and the decimation of our environment.

Yet the conflict between the pursuit of wealth and the promotion of sanity still rages on, the former benefiting from reinforcements provided by the implicit belief that wealth creation is of primary importance in the definition of progress. For centuries now, as society's hawks seek to dominate its doves, greed and power have overrun sensitivity, humility and an affinity with Nature that were the guiding principles of our species and amongst those communities studied by Weston A. Price. Nowhere is this conflict more clearly demonstrated than in the ideological confrontation between the European invaders of North America's new found lands and the indigenous inhabitants of those lands. And nowhere is this summed up more poignantly than by Price himself, at the end of his book, *Nutrition and Physical Degenera*tion.

He quotes from one Ernest Thompson Seton, the author of The Gospel of the Red Man.

"The culture and civilisation of the White man are essentially material; his measure of success is, 'How much property have I acquired for myself?' The culture of the Red man is fundamentally spiritual; his measure of success is, 'How much service have I rendered to my people?'

In common with all traditional and peaceful communities the world over, these gentle people have been portrayed as primitives and savages by avaricious invaders full of their own importance and high on the power drug. Nothing has changed, and the latter still condemn the former in justification of their own self-seeking exploitative ways. These ways must be changed, however, and balance restored, if we are to have a future.

Price's remarkable book ends in praise of the gentle approach, with a poem by Elizabeth Odell about the soul of Man and his reverence for Nature, of which he is an inextricable part.

> Flat outstretched upon a mound
> Of earth I lie; I press my ear
> Against its surface and I hear
> Far off and deep, the measured sound
> Of heart that beats within the ground.
> And with it pounds in harmony
> The swift, familiar heart in me.
> They pulse as one, together swell,
> Together fall; I cannot tell
> My sound from earth's, for I am part
> Of rhythmic, universal heart.

Further Reading

Benson, Richard : *The Farm*, Hamish Hamilton, 2005

Bywater, Michael : *Lost Worlds*, Granta Books, 2004

David, Elizabeth : *A Book of Mediterranean Food*, John Lehmann, 1950

de Selincourt, Kate : *Local Harvest*, Lawrence & Wishart, 1997

Drummond, E C, *The Englishman's Diet*, Jonathan Cape, 1959

Ehrenfeld, David : *Beginning Again*, Oxford University Press, 1993

Elliott, Robert : *The Food Maze*, Real Life Books, 2008

Enig, Mary : *Eat Fat Lose Fat*, Hudson Street Press, 2004

Fallon, Sally : *Nourishing Traditions*, New Trends Publishing, 2007

Fukuoka, Masanobu : *The One-Straw Revolution*, Rodale Press, 1978

Fukuoka, Masanobu : *The Natural Way of Farming*, Bookventure, 1993

Grigson, Jane : *The Vegetable Book*, Michael Joseph, 1978

Groves, Barry : *Trick and Treat*, Hammersmith Press, 2008

Gussow, Joan Dye : *This Organic Life*, Chelsea Green, 2001

Hodgson, Tony : *Good Food Stories*, Shepheard-Walwyn, 2006

Kendrick, Malcolm : *The Great Cholesterol Con*, John Blake, 2007

King, Franklin Hiram : *Farmers of Forty Centuries*, Dover Publications, 2004

Kingsolver, Barbara : *Animal, Vegetable, Miracle*, Harper Collins, 2007

Kneen, Brewster : *Invisible Giant*, Pluto Press, 1995

Lawrence, Felicity : *Eat Your Heart Out*, Penguin Books, 2008

Luard, Elizabeth : *The Rich Tradition of European Peasant Cookery*, Bantam Press, 1994

Mallet, Gina : *Last Chance to Eat,* McClelland & Stewart, 2004

Mabey, Richard : *Food For Free*, Collins, 1972

Orwell, George : *The Road to Wigan Pier*, Victor Gollanz, 1237

Parker-Bowles, Tom : *E Is For Eating*, Long Barn Books, 2004

Pollan, Michael : *The Omnivore's Dilemma*, Penguin, 2006

Pollan, Michael : *In Defence of Food*, Allen Lane, 2008

Ravnskov, Uffe : *The Cholesterol Myths*, New trends Publishing, 2001

Saxon, Edgar J : *Sensible Food For All*, C.W. Daniel Co, 1939

Teitel, Martin : *Rain Forest in Your Kitchen*, Island Press, 1992

Visser, Margaret : *Much Depends on Dinner*, Penguin Books, 1986

Whitley, Andrew : *Bread Matters*, Fourth Estate, 2006

Yeatman, Marwood : *The Last Food of England*, Ebury Press, 2007

Acknowledgments

In seeing this book come to life, there are a few people I would especially like to thank. Primarily, my thanks go to Sally Dean for her patience, encouragement, clarity of vision and her fearless wielding of the editor's pen. Special thanks also to my brother, Chris Elliott (www.jadeart.co.nz) for his excellent illustrations.

I would like to thank all those who have become ambassadors for the message in my writing, and those who sent me positive feedback on The Food Maze, but it would be a long list, and I would run the risk of leaving someone out. So my sincere thanks to all of you.

I thank also those people who allowed me to use this book to tell their stories: (in no particular order) Hannah Cameron and Bec Swan, Martin and Rachel Soble, Richard and Louise Eklof, Anne, Pete, Emma, Claire and Ben Cianchi, Duncan and Gail Sayce, Teresa Harris and Neville Freeman.

And last, but most definitely not least, the team at Orphans Press who all contributed to the production of this book, Andy and Helen Bowden, Steve Bowgen, Duncan Betts and of course Jerry Johns for his advice and input.